ENGLAND'S GLORY

THE MORELAND STORY

ENGLAND'S GLORY

THE MORELAND STORY

PETER CAMPION

TEMPUS

Dedicated to the memory of Terry Buss, who was passionate about the hobby of matchbox collecting, particularly England's Glory and the Moreland factory. Also to the late Sid Gwyn-Smith for his encouragement in starting this book many years ago.

Frontispiece: A view of the factory from the Bristol Road.

First published 2005

Tempus Publishing Limited
The Mill, Brimscombe Port,
Stroud, Gloucestershire, GL5 2QG
www.tempus-publishing.com

© Peter Campion, 2005

The right of Peter Campion to be identified as the Author
of this work has been asserted in accordance with the
Copyrights, Designs and Patents Act 1988.

British Library Cataloguing in Publication Data.
A catalogue record for this book is available from the British Library.

ISBN 0 7524 3567 1

Typesetting and origination by Tempus Publishing Limited.
Printed in Great Britain.

Contents

Acknowledgements

I am deeply indebted to Jim Stevenson for his untiring work in editing, organising and laying out the pictures and pages generally. Without your help Jim, I think I would have given up.

Many thanks for help go to Gloucester City Council, Gloucester Local Studies Library, Gloucester Record Office, Hackney Archives, Swedish Match, Hugh Conway-Jones, Roger Eldridge, Gavin Greenhow, Mick James, Ken Lury, Robert Moreland, Ruth and Peter Neighbour, James Oxley-Brennan, Bob Sandoe, Derek Saunders, Steven Smith, John Summers, the late David van der Plank and many other match collectors, especially Richard Tolson.

Also I am indebted to the many ex-employees of Moreland's and people of Gloucester whom I have visited and talked to over the years. They have all been most generous with information and the loan of photographs, etc.

Thanks also to the Gloucestershire Media for permission to publish photographs, etc. and especially to *The Citizen* for putting me in touch with people in Gloucestershire.

And, of course, thanks to Pam for her help and patience over many years.

Introduction
– Why Gloucester?

Gloucester was already an important port when Samuel Moreland started his timber business there in 1850, and over the next fifteen years trade obviously expanded. Because of the strength of the timber trade established in Gloucester he may have looked around at other activities to diversify or for greater profitability.

For whatever reason, Samuel decide to start match manufacturing, the first such enterprise in Gloucester. The nearest other centre of match making was Bristol, where various firms have started and finished since the 1850s, except, that is, for one small business being run by a Mr Harris from 1870, which was later to come under the control of Octavius Hunt and is still in business today under that name.

The four generations of the Moreland family in the garden of Pemberton House, Gloucester, home of the founder who was then over ninety years old. Left to right: Samuel John Moreland (founder), Harry Moreland (son), Samuel John Moreland (great-grandson and future managing director), Henry Moreland (grandson).

In 1867 Samuel Moreland took on a partner, Harry Jacobs (who probably just put up some money) and employed William Taylor to manage and start up the new venture. William, although Gloucester born, and trained as a hairdresser, is reputed to have learnt the match-making trade in Birmingham. William Taylor left Moreland sometime after the partnership with Harry Jacobs ended in 1869 and went on to manage a match works for slate merchants, Henry Belcher and Joseph Smith Gee, which started in April 1871. This was at the City Match Works, now the car park of Homebase, Lower Westgate Street. The land was owned by St Bartholomew's Hospital, which is the very pleasing stone building next door. The lease for the match works was reassigned to Henry Arnold and Thomas Gee, who was the elder brother of Joseph. Unfortunately a fire destroyed the works within a year on 23 September 1872 but public subscription enabled rebuilding and the business continued, later employing 200 people. William Taylor left after the fire and started on his own in October that year and continued his business until selling up in 1880.

Thomas Gee bought out Henry Arnold in April 1873, producing thirteen different brands, including England's Glory, until the business was taken over by S.J. Moreland in 1881.

Chapter 10, on transport, helps to explain why Gloucester was a good centre for the humble match-making business that was to become known worldwide. I suspect, however, that Samuel Moreland would have been successful in most places that had the necessary raw materials and distribution networks.

Further reading on the Gees and William Taylor can be found in the series 'Matches from Gloucester' by the author, entitled: 'William Taylor and the other match makers of the Island'.

The four generations of the Moreland family.

one

In the Beginning

Samuel John Moreland (SJM) was born in Stroud in 1828 where his father carried on the trade of sawyer (sawing timber into planks with a two-man saw or a water-driven saw). The two-man saw was operated vertically with the senior sawyer above the workpiece guiding the cut and his junior in a pit below (a most unenviable position). The family moved to Gloucester in about 1834 where his father continued in the timber trade, possibly as a clerk.

About 1850 SJM started as a lath renderer (maker of thin wooden laths for nailing to beams to support plaster for walls or ceilings). By 1853 he was advertising, at his City Saw Mill in High Orchard, Gloucester, 'Steam sawing, planing, moulding, joinery works, red and white spruce flooring, pine boards and all building timbers'. Although sawing had been tried by waterwheel some years earlier, this had largely been abandoned in favour of pit sawing, though this was about to change radically with the advent of steam mechanisation.

By 1851 the number of pit sawyers in Gloucester had risen to seventy-five pairs. The timber trade in the city was booming, mainly due to softwoods being imported from the Baltic States by sea to Bristol, then up the River Severn to Sharpness. From there smaller ships or barges would transport the timber up the Gloucester & Berkeley Canal into the city. Prepared timber and joinery products, apart from those for local use, were sent from Gloucester via the river and the expanding railways into the Midlands and other areas.

In 1851 there were 8,547 men and women in employment in the city with most employers having five or fewer workers. There were 485 bargemen and 111 seamen, which indicates the importance of the docks. Timber imports in 1856 amounted to 48,760 tons, which rose to 160,257 in 1877. Unfortunately, later on in that century the docks began a gradual decline up until the present day.

During 1854 and 1855 Messrs William Eassie, also of High Orchard, in association with Price & Co., had a contract to produce wooden huts and hospitals for the British and French armies in the Crimea, probably for the hospitals at Scutari and Balaclava. The company employed as many as a thousand men working in shifts. Undoubtedly they had a problem completing on time and so subcontracted some of the work to SJM. (One of these huts was still in use as a builders' hut at Ross on Wye in 1956.)

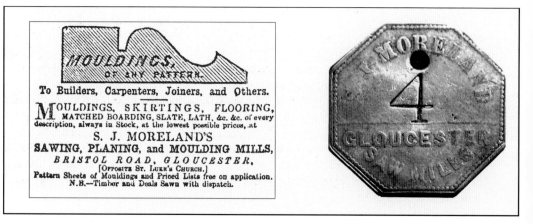

Above left: Advertisement in the Gloucester Journal in the early 1850s.

Above right: A tally was issued from the early 1850s to about 1880 to an employee requiring perhaps a tool from the stores. The number indicates the employee and the tally was retained until the return of the tool.

These huts were made by Wm Eassie & Price & Co. for British and French armies in the Crimean War, probably for hospital use.

The *Gloucester Journal* reported a violent gale, on Wednesday 23 February 1861, that damaged many properties in Gloucester including Moreland's Saw Mills, near St Luke's church, where 'the roof was much damaged and a chimney stack thrown down'.

S.J. Moreland also supplied waste wood to the match makers Bryant & May until a difference arose between them. Shortly after, on the 26 March 1867, an indenture was drawn up between SJM and an upholsterer and general dealer of Gloucester, called Harry Jacobs. Harry was quite a remarkable character; not only was he an upholsterer but also a cabinet maker, a glass and china dealer and ironmonger. His premises in Gloucester (he also had some in Cheltenham) were known as 'The Little Dustpan'. It was agreed that they were to become partners in manufacturing matches. The premises were to be adjoining the Gloucester & Berkeley Canal on a site in the Bristol Road, formerly occupied by Messrs Tredwell as engineering yards.

SJM also leased Pond Field between the canal and Bristol Road where he excavated a lie-by in front of the property, so that vessels could discharge their cargoes of timber. It is doubtful if he made much use of this area as he obtained permission to reassign the lease in 1869 to timber merchant William Nicks. The site, known as Canada Wharf, is still occupied by Nicks & Co. (Timber) Ltd today. Later that year SJM formed a timber float where the road touched the canal at Two Mile Bend between Hempstead and Quedgely.

At the start of the partnership with Harry Jacobs, William Taylor was engaged to start up and supervise the enterprise. One of his early tasks was to teach about 100 women and girls the art of box making.

The partnership only lasted a year or so and SJM bought out Harry for £1,000. The match works moved higher up the Bristol Road to a new factory in October 1868 after the partnership dissolved. This site was to serve Moreland's for over 100 years and was to expand and alter considerably in the future.

Overleaf: Tredwell's Yard, where Samuel Moreland and Harry Jacobs started their match-making business in 1867, was later to become known as Canada Wharf. (Map reproduced by courtesy of Gloucester Collection, Local Studies Library.)

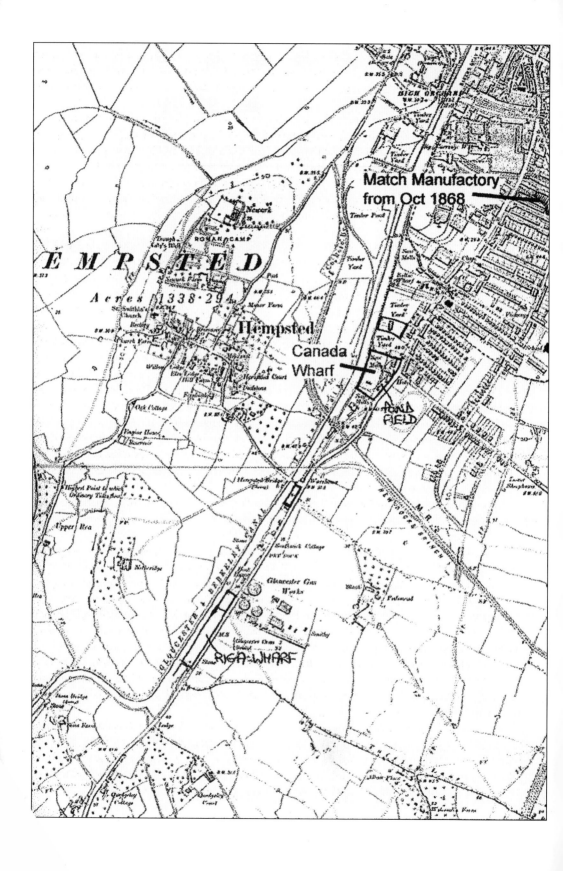

EMPSTED

Acres 1338·294

Match Manufactory
from Oct 1868

Hempsted

Canada
Wharf

POND
FIELD

RIGA WHARF

In 1869 E.W. Pickard placed a notice in the *Gloucester Journal* stating that he had purchased from SJM the City Saw Mills, Church Street, High Orchard and informed builders and merchants of the trade that he intended to carry on the same business and would welcome their custom.

Presumably, SJM then combined the sawmills and match making on the same new site in the Bristol Road. The *Gloucester Journal* reported on 23 March 1869 that SJM, proprietor of Saw Mills at Sudbrook and lucifer manufacturer, had employed a boy, Thos Jew, aged eleven, for more than seven hours; employed him on 5, 6 and 7 March after one o'clock; and also employed the boy without a school certificate. (If a child did not bring a certificate to show that he had attended school for half the previous day, the employer was then obliged to discharge him.) The charges were not pressed with severity but were found proved. SJM was ordered to pay costs of £2-3-0.

All or part of the site then known as Tredwell's Yard was taken over by Ashbee & Son in 1872 who were listed as timber merchants and joiners. The trade directories of 1873 listed them as match manufacturers but it is unlikely that they ever produced matches. I believe this listing of Ashbee was due to the previous associations of the site with Moreland's match manufacturing. Although still listed as timber merchants and/or importers up to 1883, Ashbee's last trade entries for products and for the sawmills were in 1873.

By 1871 SJM and his wife Mary, who had married in 1857, had left No.1 Cambridge Villa in Bristol Road and were living in adjacent Phillip Street with their four children. Harry, born in 1864, and Phillip, a year later, were the firm's future managers. SJM then owned six houses in adjacent Phillip Terrace and twenty-six houses in Phillip Street as well as a few others. Many more were purchased over the next several decades to house the company's employees. A row in Phillip Street was demolished in 1911 to expand the match factory.

The match works was now well established with a rateable value of £90 and employing more than 500 men, women and children making at least 360,000 boxes of matches weekly. (This equates to nearly 13½ miles if the boxes were laid end to end, or about 625 miles if the individual matches were!)

Then a gloomy article appeared in the *Gloucester Chronicle* on 29 April 1871, which has been paraphrased:

Early in April an export order to Boston was arranged but that was placed in jeopardy by Chancellor Lowe's plan to quadruple the tax on matches and fusees. Since the halfpenny tax stamp would be attached to the box before exportation, a loss of interest would occur on the capital tied up which would also apply to imports according to SJM who had visited the match manufacturers of Sweden to view and judge for himself.

The chief fear in Gloucester is that manufacture might pass into the hands of large firms. Probably Bryant & May turn out weekly five or six times that of Moreland and must, of course, have a much larger working capital. A big advantage at Gloucester is that the boxes as well as the matches are made in one factory. But with the duty imposed, the tax which has to be paid to the government weekly before the matches can leave the factory, amounts to three hundred and sixty thousand half pence or £750. Together with the wages of more than 500 hundred men, women and children it seems impossible to continue without at least £20,000 worth of capital.

Thousands of boxes of varied sizes, colour and inscriptions are piled in heaps. The Paraffin, The ruby and every type of match and fusee, apart from that known as the wax taper, are made in this factory. Now and then in a farther building there is a slight explosion as a few of the matches accidentally rub, blaze and smoke. But the system is too perfect to permit much of this. It will be a very sad day if this means of livelihood has to cease. Yet this appears to be the probable result as far as Gloucester is concerned.

Queen Victoria, concerned about the consequences of the tax, wrote to the Chancellor on the same day as a meeting of some 3,000 match workers took place in London. A petition was delivered to the House of Commons.

The demonstration march, which started peacefully, had been infiltrated by political agitators and was broken up by the police with much violence. The following day there were protests in Parliament and the Chancellor announced the withdrawal of the match tax.

Some Moreland workers listed in the 1871 census.

Name	Address	Year born	Trade	Where born
Bailey, George	4 Phillip Street	1836	Match maker	London
Bailey, Elizabeth	as above	1851		Newcastle
(Five children)				Belfast/Liverpool
Rayner, Alfred	as above	1848	Dipper	London
(Wife and child)				
Lovell, Henry	6 Phillip Street	1835	Foreman	Bethnal Green
(Wife and four children)				
Laws, Francis	23 Phillip Street	1857	Match maker	Gloucester
Ward, John	25 Phillip Street	1850	Match maker	Spitafields, London
Gibson, Robert	26 Phillip Street	1858	Works at factory	Bristol
O'Brien, Anne	6 Little Norfolk Street	1851	Matchbox maker	Gloucester
Hartland, Elizabeth	28 Sherborne Street	1852	Works at factory	Gloucester
Hartland, William	as above	1855	Works at factory	Gloucester
Sturge, Tom	25 Alma Place	1855	Match sorter	Gloucester
Kilminster, Eliz	3 Clarence Town	1855	Match sorter	Gloucester
Kilminster, Maria	as above	1854	Match sorter	Gloucester
McMallan, Ann	Alma Place		Match sorter	Belfast

two

A near disaster

An alarming fire on 13 October 1876 was reported by the *Gloucester Journal*:

The premises comprise of two long parallel rows of low brick buildings running at right angles to the Bristol Road, and connected by a cross row at the further end, thus forming three sides of an oblong.

The row of buildings at the southern side is used for storing the wood to be made into matches, and here also the wood is cut into splints, a steam engine for that purpose being stationed at the further end. The cross row comprises of five drying rooms, each 30ft long, 12ft wide and 15ft high, in which the splints are spread to dry before being dipped in brimstone. These drying rooms are heated by steam pipes from the engine boiler at one end of the row. The northern side of the oblong consists of buildings in which the splints are dipped, placed in boxes and stored for despatch. It was in the cross row, used for drying purposes that the fire broke out.

Work finished at the factory at around 5pm on Thursday and the premises were left about half past nine by Mr Henry Payne, the foreman, apparently quite safe. Between one and two o'clock the following morning, Mr Griffin, DCC, [Deputy Chief Constable] who was returning from a country round, passed the buildings and saw nothing to attract attention. Wood, the policeman on beat, to whom Mr Griffin then spoke, also reported all safe in the neighbourhood. Very soon after – about half past two – one of the drying rooms was discovered to be on fire.

PC Wood raised the alarm, and with their usual promptitude, the three Gloucester engines – the London, Liverpool and Globe, the Norwich and the Phoenix – with their respective staffs, were very quickly on the spot. Mr Griffin, to whom the news reached while at the Cross just as he was finishing his nightly round, came to the scene with Sergeants Piff and Mathews and a force of policemen. But for a while firemen and police alike were powerless. There was no water.

The Bristol Road district depends, for its water, principally upon the waterworks constructed by the Rev. Canon Lysons at Hempstead, and at night the supply from these works is cut off. So for a considerable period – difficult to estimate accurately for in scenes of excitement one loses count of time – the fire blazed away unchecked. The inflammable nature of the material – wood dried especially for ignition – caused the flames to burn with great fierceness. Fanned by a high wind, and apparently increased in fury by the rain which all the while fell in torrents, lurid tongues of fire shot high into the air, illuminating the district for miles around and scattering showers of sparks in a most alarming manner. The liveliest of fears were entertained lest the inflammable stores, in the other portions of the establishment, should ignite in which case the whole premises must have been consumed.

Meanwhile the firemen were at their wits end for water. The city supply, turned on at the first alarm, ends at the level crossing and was therefore too far off to be available. The canal water was useless for a similar reason; and the contents of a pond, near the canal, proved too much like mud to be passed through the hose. At length somebody by 'happy thought' remembered a good well on adjacent premises and to this access was speedily obtained and the engines went to work with a will.

The flames had spread from the drying rooms to an engine house adjoining, but here the efforts of the firemen succeeded in checking them and a part of the engine house was saved. The drying rooms and contents were totally burnt out before the fire could be said to be under control about daybreak. The rest of the premises, thanks probably to the heavy rain, remained untouched.

According to the *Gloucester Journal* report:

…the fire was probably caused by splints coming into contact with a hot pipe in the drying room or a match may have been accidentally dropped by a worker. The goods valued at about £550 were in process of manufacture and so were not liable to insurance compensation. Damage to the premises amounted to some £500 which was covered by insurance.

In this, as in almost every other instance of fire in Gloucester, there seems to be but little doubt that the fire could have been extinguished with little trouble had water been at once accessible.

The credit of preventing a boiler explosion, from the heat and burning premises, is due to a labourer named Frederick Broom who, with great presence of mind, turned off the steam from the engine soon after the alarm was given.

SJM's son Harry joined the firm in 1880 and was soon followed by his brother Philip. It was Harry who realized the value of advertising and with his business acumen made a great success of the commercial running of the business.

Philip went to Sweden to study the engineering and logistics of the match trade. His Swedish dictionary survives today dated late 1880s. He was an inventive genius and became a fine engineer, devoting his energies to the machinery and practical side of the works, including designing the matches. He dealt with any mechanical problems, made improvements and developed new machinery, some of which was patented.

During the next two decades or so, Henry and Philip built on the success of their father, and the company, with a firm foundation, made great progress. By 1885 the firm was employing over 1,000 outworkers making boxes for matches.

In 1882 SJM added '& Sons' to the match labels, but not all the old stock of boxes were withdrawn and were still being issued whilst they lasted. Harry and Philip were taken into partnership with their father in 1890.

The brothers were keen fishermen and both laid claim to a single 'penny farthing' cycle. When going out on such a trip, these two young men would, each in turn, ride the cycle for a mile or so and then drop it in a hedge and walk on. The other would find it, then take his turn at riding on before leaving it again for his brother.

Above: England's Glory label, *c.*1893–94.

Right: Gee's label, *c.*1873–80, with HMS *Warrior* – extremely rare.

About 1882 the first serious brand name, 'England's Glory', appeared (according to Ivan Pritchard; however, in fact it was probably eight or nine years later), taking over the name from the earlier manufacturer Thomas Gee of Gloucester. Moreland's, who are thought to have purchased the firm of Thos Gee around 1880, also adopted some other brands used by Gee. In 1891 the England's Glory label design was officially registered, but much altered from Gee's label, and was printed in black on light yellow paper instead of Gee's plain sepia. Colour for the England's Glory label started in 1898.

The use of England's Glory as a brand name had great patriotic appeal, as did Jack Tar and John Bull. It turned out to be a brilliant stroke and the brand name England's Glory is still remembered and known by people today who may have no idea by whom or where these matches were made.

According to Moreland's records, Queen Victoria decreed that, for patriotic reasons, only England's Glory matches were to be used in Royal households. This may have helped in a small way, but imports of cheap matches continued from abroad and were responsible for the closure of some machines in the factory, and they were to have other far-reaching consequences in later years.

Flyer announcing the lucky winners of the 1896 model competition.

By 1880 Moreland was the only match manufacturer left in Gloucester. There had been the slate merchants Belcher, Gee & Co., who started the new City Match Works in April 1871, with William Taylor as manager sometime after he had left Moreland's. Then came Arnold, Gee & Co., taken over by Thomas Gee, and finally William Taylor gave up his own works to manage a pub. For further information on all the Gloucester match manufacturers at this time, with the exception of Moreland's, refer to the booklet 'Matches from Gloucester' by the same author published in 1986.

Most of the sales around 1890 were achieved in the working class districts of the north, the west, the Midlands and Northern Ireland. Ingenious ideas were introduced to increase trade. In 1896 there were competitions advertised at Gloucester and Great Charles Street, Birmingham depot, for those that could send in the greatest number of empty England's Glory boxes. Prizes ranged from Humber bicycles (then worth £23 each) to engraved silver watches or even £50 cash.

There were also prizes of furniture, clothing, jewellery, etc. for collecting specific numbers of dozen wrappers. Later in 1930 a box camera could be exchanged for 425 wrappers; an oak upholstered armchair required 1,300 wrappers; while at the top of the list you had to save 3,000 wrappers for a silver fob watch. (Considering each wrapper would have contained a dozen boxes

Flyer for distribution of watches and bicycles for the greatest number of empty England's Glory boxes sent in between 27 February and 2 March 1897.

of matches, if a family used one box per day it would have taken them over ninety-eight years to obtain the silver fob watch – providing the competition was still in operation by then!)

Another type of competition was for model making, as described by the *Strand Magazine* in 1898 with the majority of the article reproduced here.

Two or three years ago Moreland's hit upon the excellent idea of getting up public competitions on entirely original lines. Of course, the firm's primary motive was the sale and general advertisement of their wares; but they also considered how they could best tap the wonderful fund of originality which they knew the average British workman does possess.

It was at length resolved that the competition should take the form of model making 'the greatest novelty of any sort that can be made with not less than 1,000 of our matchboxes'. The conditions were widely advertised in Birmingham and its environs. Competent judges – architects chiefly - were appointed. The first prize was £50, the second £25, third £10, and then came three other prizes of £5 each. In subsequent competitions, however, the amounts were slightly varied, but in all cases the prize money aggregated £100. Models were to be sent carriage paid to the Birmingham depot, and those exhibits winning a prize became

A page from the book of prizes for the wrapper competitions.

the absolute property of the firm. Later on Moreland's hired a shop in Birmingham for the express purpose of exhibiting to the public the prize-winning models.

Here is shown a representative collection of photographs of these 'marvels in matchboxes'. In some cases the model occupied the spare time of its creator for six months or more; and the effect of the whole was heightened by clockwork arrangements and similar contrivances.

It is to Moreland's Birmingham manager, Mr George Blakely, that we are indebted for most of the photographs.

The wonderful piano seen in the first photograph is actually full size, being 5ft in height, and constructed entirely of matchboxes, which, according to the rules of the competition, must have contained Moreland's wares. The instrument was awarded first prize in the third competition, so that it may be said to have fetched the price of a real cottage piano. The judges were Messrs Gamely and Parsons, well-known architects in Birmingham. The maker of the piano was Mr G.W. Roberts, of Birmingham. Mr Roberts served as tuner for many years with the well-known house of Broadwood, so that a piano suggested itself naturally to him. He used upwards of 3,200 ordinary matchboxes, and 576 boxes that had contained small wax-vestas. The only other thing he used was 5lb of glue.

To increase sales many advertising schemes were used; 3,000 wrappers from a pack of a dozen matchboxes could be exchanged for this silver pocket watch.

Made from almost 4,000 Moreland's boxes, this model was 5ft tall and won first prize.

Originality seems to run in the Roberts family, for we next show a marvellous model of the great Laxey Wheel, in the Isle of Man, made by Miss L.W. Roberts, sister to the designer of the piano. 'The Laxey Wheel', writes Mr Roberts, 'was 6ft in length and 4ft high. It took a little less than six months to make, and used up about 3,000 matchboxes.'

In some cases more than one competitor took the same original for his model. For instance, the Laxey Wheel was also adopted by Mr James Shaw, of Nottingham. Mr Shaw's model, which won the first prize, was no less than 6ft 7in in height, 2ft in depth, and 8ft in length. It contained 4,500 boxes, and took five months to complete. The wheel itself was 5ft 6in in diameter, and went by clockwork. Another competitor, Mr Lewis Sheldon, of Winson Green, Birmingham, constructed a double-masted turret ship-of-war, 8ft 3in long. The completeness of this model was astonishing; the ship carried fifteen guns (all made out of matchboxes), and there were six lifeboats.

The next two models shown are the work of Mr F. Marshall, of Sneinton, Nottingham. The first of Mr Marshall's models depicted gained the third prize in the second competition. It is a very faithful reproduction of the Forth Bridge, and is, of course, made entirely out of matchboxes.

The Laxey Wheel on the Isle of Man.

The Forth Bridge, which won third prize, was 10ft 6in long, made entirely from matchboxes and withstood a test weight of 42lb in the centre of each arch.

The height of the model is 1ft 10in, the width 12in, and the length no less than 10ft 6in. The model contained about 3,000 boxes.

'Other than matchboxes', writes Mr Marshall, 'no material whatever is used in the construction of the bridge - not even in the stays. When completed it stood the test of 42lb weight in the centre of either arch. I never saw the original bridge, but got an idea of it from a lithograph in a railway guide. The model contains 241 stays and twelve principal pillars. Seven rows of matchboxes form the roadway over the bridge, and on this roadway are laid the sleepers and rails.'

Mr Marshall's second model is what is known as an Eiffel bicycle. When complete, this model was in full working order. It contains 1,100 matchboxes, and stands a little more than 6ft in height. The diamond stays

Also by Mr Marshall was the working Eiffel bicycle with a 9ft long chain made from matchbox sides glued to tape.

are two boxes thick. The driving chain is 9ft long, and was made from the sides of the matchbox drawers glued onto tape. The wheels are 24in in diameter.

Another model of Mr Marshall's was a reproduction of the lighthouse near New Brighton. This model was fitted with a revolving lantern, and the whole contained 2,900 matchboxes.

The next model reproduced is a highly elaborate affair, made by Mr Grubb, of Atherstone. This is supposed to represent Nelson's famous ship Victory passing a large lighthouse. As will be seen, the ship, the lighthouse, and the entire background, with its wings, are all composed of matchboxes. Working three hours a night, Mr Grubb finished his model in five months. The ship is 3ft 6in long; and the lighthouse, 5ft 2in high, and nearly 2ft square. To build a circular lighthouse, with the awkward material at his disposal, was a little beyond Mr Grubb. The designer, it should be said, is very well acquainted with nautical matters, having served as steward for some years on board a little vessel of 400 tons. Thus it will be seen that each competitor prudently followed his own bent.

The next matchbox model shown is an even more elaborate and ambitious original design, worked out by Mr Joseph Bray, also of Atherstone. 'It is a tower with elevated circular railway, made with 1,120 empty matchboxes. This was entered in Messrs Morelands' competition held last January, and gained the fourth

This model of the *Victory* took five months to build spending three hours every evening.

This elevated model railway was a very elaborate affair with working electric lights.

prize of £10. The model was 36in long, 39in high, and 24in wide. The boxes were put together with glue, and the model was very firm and substantial. I worked upon it at night after I had finished my day's work. You will see that even the foundation of the platform is made of matchboxes. The bottom of the tower is supposed to contain shops and it has four entrances and sixteen windows. The railway track around the tower was laid with rails and sleepers, and a clockwork train was run upon it at intervals. The platform for the station is on the right-hand side of the model, where I also built a booking-office and signal-box with levers. On the left-hand side are a promenade, a bandstand, and a railway station with a refreshment room. These buildings were all worked round with brass wire, so as to represent railings, and the whole model had small lamps for electric lights.'

The next matchbox model to be shown is one representing the stately old red-brick gateway of St James's Palace, as viewed from St James's Street. You will see from the label that it gained the fourth prize of £10. It is the work of Mr J.K. Round, of Dudley.

Mr Round's model contained 2,380 common matchboxes and 620 wax-vesta boxes. He took particular note of the time occupied in its construction – 106 hours. From the ground to the top of the flag on the tower measured no less than 6ft 4in. The clock was a real one, working twenty-four hours with one winding. The dial had a diameter of 8in. The dial, with figures and hands, were made of parts of the inevitable matchbox. There was a motto surrounded by flowers, 'Long live the Queen'. It only remains to be said that both the letters and flowers were made from bits of matchbox or the paper covering thereon. Yet another of these wonderful little models. This design is an ideal one, and is supposed to represent a desirable 'Home for Old Soldiers and Sailors'. Upwards of 3,000 matchboxes were used in the construction of this model, and it was made in its designer's spare time after he had worked ten hours a day at his own occupation. This model is

This gateway of St James's Palace, with a working clock, took 106 hours to build.

Above: Mr Jordan spent 1,000 hours on this home with just an old razor, glue and of course matchboxes.

Right: The Great Wheel of Earl's Court won first prize.

the work of Mr Evan H. Jordan, of Cheadle, Staffs. Mr Jordan says, 'It took me about a thousand hours; the only things I used were an old razor and a pot of glue.'

A particularly good and accurate representation of the Great Wheel at Earl's Court is next reproduced. This model gained a first prize of £50. Mr S. Jennings, of Walsall, was the designer. The wheel contains 2,110 matchboxes, every one of which had to be cut, carved, and dovetailed into shape. The wheel has twenty-four cars, and each car has eight windows made out of mica. By a clockwork arrangement the wheel will work for fifteen minutes after being wound up. The model is 4ft high; and Mr Jennings tells me that no fewer than 500 of his neighbours came to see it at his house.

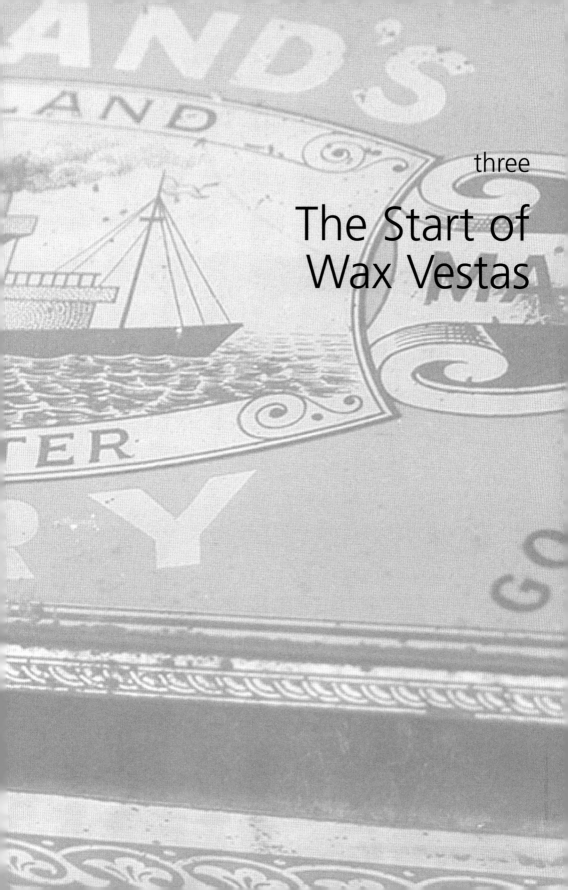

three

The Start of Wax Vestas

During 1897 wax vesta production started and the following year the first quantity of wax vestas was exported to Australia. Other exports were to Canada and South Africa. (The John Bull label marked with 'Average 55 matches' of paraffin matches was exported to Australia *c.*1912.) At trade exhibitions gold medals were won at Birmingham in June, Portsmouth in August and Sheffield in December. Business was also being conducted with Octavius Hunt, the Bristol match maker in this year.

In this period about 450 people were employed at the factory; the biggest department was the one for making boxes, employing 200 girls to hand fill the boxes. The factory was well laid out, being able to handle materials and goods in the proper sequence and so mostly avoiding the danger of accidents. Power for splint and box making and the hot-air drying

Left: England's Glory box of Wax Vestas, *c.*1900.

Below: Rare Wax Vesta gross label, *c.*1897–1900 (16.5 x 21cm).

machines came from two steam engines, which were run by burning the waste timber and bark.

Reproduced is part of an article that appeared in the *British Trade Journal* written following a visit to the factory in 1897:

The manufacture of vestas:
The cotton which forms the base is wound in lengths of 4,000 or 5,000 yards upon two large drums, each about 8ft in diameter, and made to revolve by steam power. The coating of stearine or wax is applied by passing this cotton through a vat filled with the molten material and placed midway between the two drums. As these revolve the cotton is unwound from one and rewound upon the other, and this is done a number of times, or until each hank is thoroughly saturated and well coated.

In this process we noticed that the cotton is divided into hanks, each consisting of twenty-six threads. This determines the thickness the vesta is to have. Vestas differ greatly in the thickness and finish of the wax and number of threads employed. The ordinary vesta consists of only sixteen or twenty threads, is poorly coated and has a coarse, rough surface. The result is that such a vesta burns for less than a minute and is easily bent or broken. England's Glory Vestas may be put to the severest tests and they come out very successfully. Their greater thickness enables them to burn with a large strong flame for the space of about a minute and a half.

When the cotton has been well coated it is rolled onto a smaller drum, from which it passes into a cutting machine. This chops it into vesta lengths which are at the same time fixed into frames for dipping.

This is done in an adjoining building using the same principle applied to wood matches. Each length of wax taper being held into the striking composition until the ends of the cotton are well covered with the mixture.

The frames, still with the vestas fixed, are placed in a drying room and from there to the box filling department, where girls are surrounded by boxes of cardboard, wood and tin. These are rapidly filled with the vestas and sent to the packing rooms where they are packed into gross and half gross boxes. They are produced in a variety of sizes ranging from the small half penny box to the large tin box for the smoke room table. Many designs are embellished with attractive photographs while the most prominent of all is the England's Glory label and trademark consisting of a representation of a British man-o'-war.

The filling room is one of the largest departments in the works. About 200 girls are employed in filling the boxes with matches while a separate room is set aside for the Irish trade, which requires a special size and shape of box.

Boxes are made from thin strips of wood or from cardboard or tin plate. All, apart from the tin boxes, are made on the premises.

Machines are at work cutting the veneer into pieces for the parts of boxes. The wood, once divided and scored, is passed to a set of paper covering and pasting machines and converted into finished boxes. In one room we counted no less than forty machines turning out arrays of boxes in wood and card, already covered and labelled for the trip to the drying ovens.

Throughout the box making departments there is a large consumption of paste. The ground floor department for making the paste uses, as its raw material, about two tons of flour a week.

In order that no material shall be wasted, all odd pieces of wood which cannot be made into boxes or splints are used for making spills or pipe lights and sold to the tobacconist trade.

Larger pieces of wood, which would otherwise be useless, are worked up into elastic web boards, and quite a large room is set aside for finishing these boards, which are made in various sizes and patterns.

They are then sent to Nottingham, Leicester and other textile centres to be filled with web, lace, ribbons and similar goods.

One of two Vesta tins 16 x 8.5 and 16 x 4.5cm.

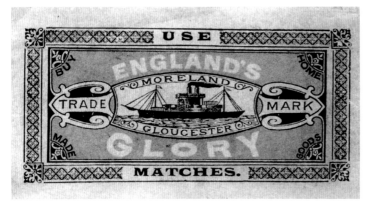

Factory label 1900–1904. On the reverse, the following is printed in addition to dotted lines for the consignee's name and address: 'From... S.J. Moreland & Sons, Manufacturers of Paraffin, Safety and Wax Matches, Braided Lights, Spills, Chip Boxes, Wood Wool, etc. Gloucester.'

"These Matches are sold by us on the distinct understanding that you are not to sell them under the following prices :—

1-31 gross - **1/8** per gross nett.

Case lots - **1/7½** „ „ "

S. J. MORELAND & SONS.

Distributor's notice c.1900–1905. This is an incredible insight to the reason why match workers were paid such low wages. In order to compete with foreign imports the cost of manufacture had to be kept down. In today's currency this was 144 boxes for approximately nine new pence. It is worth considering the price at which Moreland's sold them to the distributor.

four

The New Century

In 1904 mechanisation was such that one machine could turn sheets of wood of the correct thickness into splints at the rate of 12 million in one hour, resulting in a rough piece of timber becoming a match in this time. Another machine could produce 700 boxes an hour, which gives an idea of the production capabilities of the factory. Manufacture included vesta, safety, paraffin and vesuvian matches, as well as some wooden products. Ice-cream spoons, balls for coconut shies, skittles and garden labels were still made up to the early 1930s.

One journal on industrial Gloucester at this time records that upwards of 1,000 operatives were working at the factory, whilst the city maintained a population of 48,000. With increasing demand, constant improvements and expansion were taking place all the time. By now, the premises, including the timber yards on the canal side, occupied some six acres. The factory boasted electric lighting, an automatic fire sprinkler, ventilation and heating systems, as well as its own manufacturing, maintenance, carpentry and printing departments.

In 1906 Moreland's exported eighteen cases of safety matches to America, and at this time was also selling raw materials to match makers R. Bell & Co. of Bromley, London.

Although the works were well ventilated and managed, 1907 was the year that Thomas Davis died from phosphorus necrosis. This was a disease that could be contracted from the prolonged use of, and exposure to, white phosphorus, which made the bones very brittle, leading to necrosis, or fracture, from a very slight blow or fall. Its common name was 'phossy jaw' and entered the jaw through the teeth. Quite often match workers suffered from disintegration of the jaw bone, which naturally caused great pain and suffering. Regular dentistry had been compulsory on a quarterly basis at Gloucester but the company also carried out, for some time prior to this accident, monthly examinations.

Wooden box of spills, 1880s.

A corner of the power station, showing one of the three power units (a vertical high-speed gas engine coupled to an electrical generator). Part of the firm's refrigerating plant can be seen on the left-hand side (used for air conditioning).

Mr Davis had worked in the industry for twelve years in Ireland (the factory closed in 1901) before coming to Moreland's in 1900 as a labourer. In 1902 he had a minor accident and fractured his leg, which did not set, and was later amputated at the thigh. He was given seated work at a dipping machine, but, because of his disability, he had difficulty leaving his station to wash his hands when soiled. This, coupled with the habit of chewing tobacco, seemed to account for the phosphorous being transferred to his mouth.

He had a tooth extracted in October 1906 and resumed work after three and a half weeks; being suspended three weeks later with a slight swelling. A week later a tooth became loose and on extraction necrosis was found. He was treated at home by a surgeon appointed by Moreland's but died on 19 January 1907.

An inspection was made of the factory on 14 February 1907 by the Assistant Under-Secretary of State and the Chief Inspector of Factories. Their report to the Secretary of State spoke of 640 employees of whom 256 were engaged in the boxing of dry matches. Great detail was given of the various processes engaged but generally there was little the works could do to improve on their procedures at the time.

It was also stated that Mr Davis had worked in the industry for many years before much consideration was given to the welfare of employees and undoubtedly the onset of necrosis had started before his arrival at Gloucester.

Moreland's had additionally been using the name Gloucester Match Company for some years to market matches (more information is contained in the appendix of this book and in the booklet 'Gloucester Match Company' by the same author, published in 1995 but currently out of print). The only brand to be registered under the name of Gloucester Match was 'As used by Conn' in 1911.

Samuel Moreland finally handed over to his sons, Harry and Philip, in 1910 and died at the age of ninety-six in 1924. He was energetic, tough and strong willed but also fair minded and lived for his match factory.

33/712

TRADE MARKS ACT, 1905.

Additional Representation of Trade Mark, to Accompany Application for Registration (other than Cotton Mark).

3 0 MAY. 1911

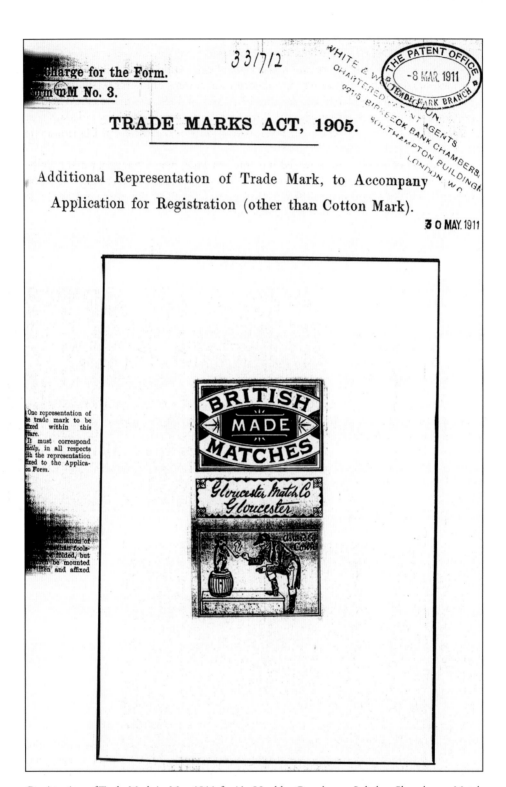

Registration of Trade Mark in May 1911 for 'As Used by Conn' – see Labels – Shaughraun Match.

The *Gloucester Journal* at the time said: 'He deserves to be remembered with the greatest respect and gratitude as one of the makers of modern Gloucester. Mr Moreland is the last of a band of contemporaries to whose memories the citizens can never be sufficiently grateful.'

Extensive rebuilding had taken place in 1911, and in 1912 the first continuous automatic match-making machine was installed at Gloucester. This revolutionised the processes previously undertaken by fifteen to twenty operatives, where most of the work was laboriously done by hand.

Cut lengths of wood were now fed into the machine, which transformed the timber into matchsticks and carried them through hot paraffin wax to make the sticks burn well. The sticks then had their ends dipped into the chemical mixture to form the heads and finally dropped into ready-made boxes at the end of the machine.

This is believed to be the first picture, taken in about 1910, of Sammy's Angels, who were named after Samuel Moreland. It must have been a special occasion for the young ladies to be photographed and each certainly turned out in her Sunday best. The picture was published in the 1980s, loaned by Mrs V. Bonner, who treasured it as it includes her mother Louisa Willetts.

A view of the label and wrapper printing department. Paper slitting machines can also be seen.

Another view of match-making machines taken in 1927.

Match head composition being mixed in the chemical department to a precise consistency!

five

1913 Onwards

Probably, to the staff at Moreland's, 1913 was not a great year of change – if any change was noticed at all. However, to the Moreland family it certainly was an eventful year.

I have not come across any hint of financial difficulties, in fact the opposite, as it appears that the factory was doing well and business was good.

The firm became a limited company on 19 April 1913 and registered as S.J. Moreland & Sons Ltd with its first board meeting on 24 April at 16 Eastcheap, London. Harry and Philip Moreland were directors with Harry Grimes, of Gloucester, as secretary and solicitor. Harry and Philip held one share each with James Frederick Bond holding 274,998 shares (presumably on behalf of Bryant & May). Mr Bond also held, in his name on behalf of the company, shares in Geo. Judd Bros Ltd and Matches Ltd to the value of £3,108-5s-5d.

After the inaugural board meeting, the directors and solicitors attended the bank and paid in £275,000 (value of the share sales) and drew a cheque for the same to pay the vendors (S.J. Moreland & Sons). The secretary then paid in £1 to keep the bank account open. The registered office was at the factory in Bristol Road.

Documents at Gloucester Record Office show that the company formation was for the purpose of acquisition by Bryant & May Ltd, while the management and day-to-day running of the company would continue to be conducted by the Moreland family. Robert Moreland explained the acquisition as being tied up with events within the Match Makers Association.

The UK Match Makers Association was originally formed in 1872 by eleven members, which included Mr Bryant and Henry Arnold of Gloucester. Thomas Gee and S.J. Moreland joined in December 1873. The Association was disbanded in August 1878 and the funds went to the North Eastern Hospital for Children.

The reformed Match Makers Association held its seventh meeting in 1891. Its main function was to ensure that members did not undercut each other's price (highly illegal nowadays). In July 1900 Moreland's and Diamond Match were described by the Association as 'being very troublesome' for selling about 15 per cent below the Association prices.

Moreland's and Diamond had been invited to attend the October meeting of 1900 but did not reply. Minutes of the Association were continued after this date but are privately owned and I could not gain access to them. Robert Moreland's explanation of the sale was that it took place because of the special relationship between the family and the Bryant & May board.

In September Philip resigned from the board, retiring to pursue his outdoor interests and also to run the fishery, which had been purchased around 1900. Fishing played an important part with the family who owned the fishing rights on part of the River Wye. Harry Grimes took Philip's place as director with Henry Moreland, Harry's son, becoming secretary. During this period Philip lent Bryant & May £3,000 at 4.5 per cent and another £2,000 later in September. These loans were common practice over the following years between Moreland, Bryant & May, Midland Match and Standard Match of Gloucester, purchased by Moreland in 1926.

The first full share holding list I have seen is of May 1924, which shows members of the family, and others, with a combined holding of 26,898 shares. George Potter and Ernest Raybould held 248,102 – presumably on behalf of Bryant & May.

Looking at the company minutes of 19 December 1913, Mr Grimes states that a firm of solicitors had written about a man who was making a claim for injury received from an allegedly improperly packed box of matches, saying that their client would accept £10 in full settlement. The board considered the amount excessive and instructed one of the company travellers to call and see the man to assess the situation. Unfortunately, I have been unable to find any record of the outcome of the dispute.

Harry Moreland and his friend G. Blakely during a day's fishing, almost certainly on the River Wye.

The working week in 1913 was fifty-nine hours and the works had nineteen steam engines running to provide the required power, the fuel coming from the Forest of Dean.

Seven houses were purchased in Clifton Road for between £200–250 each without the company name being mentioned. (This information in a newspaper implied that the price would have risen if the identity of the purchaser had been known.) More houses were purchased over the following years in Clifton Road, Philip Street and Bristol Road. In February 1924, No.20 Clifton Road was bought for £500 and let out to someone at the works for 5/- per week.

Life could be hard at times, especially for the six or more boys aged twelve or so, employed by Moreland's full time in 1913. Their duties were to jump into the canal and push logs from the pond float where they were stored, across the canal to the other bank opposite the works, where they were then picked up and taken to the works for peeling into veneers the thickness of a matchstick. The logs were kept in the canal, as they had to be peeled wet, otherwise a continuous veneer could not be taken off. The pay was 2/6d a week in all weathers all the year round!

One lad with eight brothers and sisters did it for two years. His father took the 2/6d off him, saying it was too much money for him. He subsequently left and got a job at Cadbury's chocolate factory. The father later had a terminal illness and was given notice to quit the Moreland-owned house, so the daughter had to leave a well-paid job at a hotel in order to keep on the tenancy or they would all have been homeless.

Like the boys, young girls of this age were also employed. They worked in the factory filling matchboxes and at other labour-intensive work.

In August 1914 Mr Landvutter was appointed works manager at £600 a year. Supplies of potash until then were being imported from Germany. Sales for the six months to 31 August 1914 were £71,943 for matches and £621 for firewood and sundries.

The continuous production system was to be of great benefit during the First World War – an experience that was far from 'great' for the many men living in rat infested holes in the ground in another land, often up to their knees in mud and scared out of their minds; no doubt a situation that some Moreland employees suffered, as there were sixty-five employees who fought in the armed services, thirteen of whom were killed.

On the home front there were immediate difficulties in the supply of raw materials. The war had started rather unexpectedly and there had been no time to stockpile materials. Not only was timber in very short supply but chlorate of potash, at the time almost exclusively a German product, was an essential ingredient of match making. The old kelp industry was revived to make the chemical from seaweed.

A new splint conveyor was purchased in 1915 for £700, but due to the shortage of men, girls were now employed on the machines. Output was reduced whilst they learnt to use the machines. Wages were increased due to a rise in the cost of living and the usual bonus of £50 was voted to be continued to be paid to staff. Times must have still been profitable as this year £5,000 was invested with the Canadian Government and £5,000 with the Queensland Government.

The first match tax was imposed in 1916. In spite of all the improvisations of the match industry, there were acute match shortages during the war due to shortages of materials.

In June 1916 Premier Match was purchased for £1,351 and 379 shares in W.J. Morgan were purchased for £1,927. The purchase of Midland Match followed in 1919. During December

The First World War tablet engraved with the sixty-five names of Moreland's employees who served for their country, thirteen of whom did not return. The plaque is situated on the rear wall of St Stephen's church, Bristol Road.

Section of the Bonded Warehouse. Each case represents £6 13s 4d. Excise duty, which had to be paid on leaving the works, involved a lot of financial outlay for the Government's benefit.

1916, Thomas Charlton was appointed as works manager. (Three years later he left to start up Standard Match Co. Ltd with David John Smith, a commercial salesman, also of Moreland's, and Gloucester contractor William Hobrough.) Hobrough & Co. built a new power plant at the Moreland works in 1917 at a cost of £2,260.

In 1919, after years of restrictions and shortages, more extensions to the factory were erected but trade conditions were not good after the war. Costs and unemployment were rising and so was the import of cheaper foreign matches, which, due to their favourable exchange rates, could be sold wholesale for less than British-made matches.

Matters became worse with the depression after the Wall Street crash in 1929. In this year 108 machines were idle and the working week was reduced to thirty-seven and a half hours to try to keep everyone on. Unemployment in Britain went up to three million.

Neither was the match tax helpful. Two Excise Officers had an office on the premises and the tax had to be paid on the finished matches before they left the factory.

The supply of Baltic timber dried up in 1929 due to the world money crisis and parcels of black poplar, known as aspen, were bought from English and Welsh land owners and accounted for 12 per cent of the timber supplied. Logs were soaked and cut into 30in lengths at mills on the left of the Bristol Road, near Hempstead Bridge.

Otherwise it was mostly Canadian poplar from Ontario and New Brunswick through the St Lawrence and Nova Scotia ports. One shipment came from Port Churchill on the Hudson Bay.

Nothing was wasted. Short match cuttings went to button manufacturers who used them for polishing buttons.

The power house switchboard in 1927.

A wonderful photograph of a Swedish ship unloading timber at Gloucester in the early 1900s.

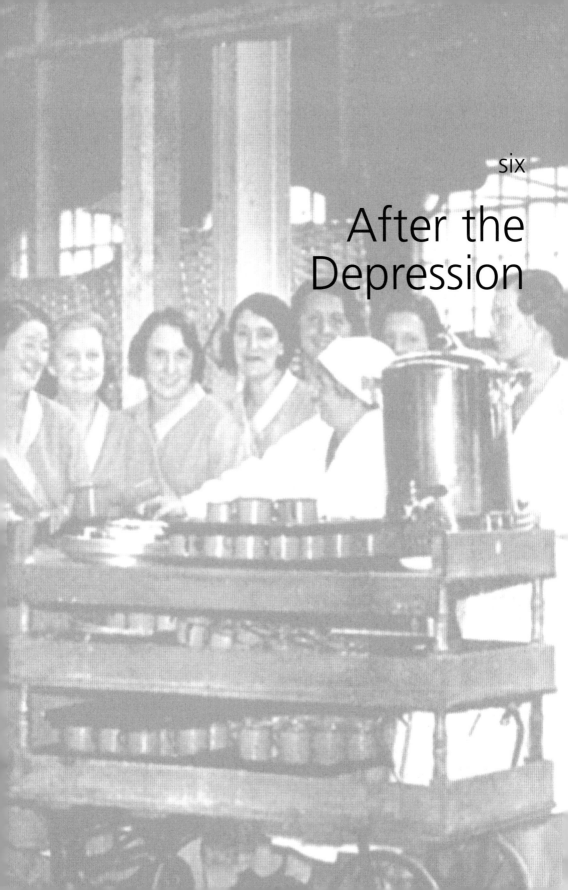

six

After the
Depression

Normality slowly returned to the country. Commercial life went on.

Many carnivals, exhibitions and agricultural shows were attended with floats to increase local sales and spread the brand names.

Following an article in The *Gloucester Citizen*, I was privileged to meet some of the employees who started in the late 1920s at Moreland's.

All the people I spoke to, around the year 2000, remarked on the fact that you had to work hard at Moreland's but if you were a good employee, the family looked after you well. No one I spoke to regretted working there even if they did not enjoy the job they performed.

I am indebted to the following for talking to me and reminiscing about their life and time spent at Moreland's: Mrs Gutsell, Mr D. Holton, Mrs Jones, Mr E. Moulden, Miss Vera Rastall, Mrs Beatrice Thomas (*née* Smith), Mr Clary Tranter, Miss Lena Turk and Mr Roy Wood. I am also indebted to those who wrote to me, namely: Mrs C. Darby (*née* Ballard), Mrs Kelly, Mrs Wendy Organ (*née* Whitehead) who wrote from Australia, and Mrs June Lohman; also to the lady who rang me up from America!

Apologies to anyone I may have missed out or whose name I have spelt incorrectly. I have moved house twice since and some of my notes are now not too easy to decipher!

Beatrice Smith started at Moreland's in 1923, working in the box-making department. In her words:

Mrs Jones, in her younger days, dressed as John Bull for a carnival float.

'Mr Harry was a tartar and everything had to be just so. When he was doing his rounds all the factory staff were aware of the fact. He was also very fair and kind, having a lot of regard for his employees. At my work I had to stand on a platform putting in the trays of matches. One morning the foreman, Mr Davis, came and asked if I was wearing stockings. The Governor had thought, on his round earlier, that I was not wearing them. "Well, I'm sorry", I replied indignantly, "but I certainly am." What was he peering at my legs for in any case?' she added.

Beatrice could remember SJM.

Mr Harry would also do a Monday morning round making sure that all were wearing clean shoes and overalls. The bosses all wore bowler hats until Mr Harry died when the tradition ceased.

Lena Turk started in 1926 and remembers that girls handling match cases had to wrap tape round their fingers to prevent the sand paper wearing their fingers raw. Previously to working at Moreland's she had earned 5/9d for a forty-eight hour week but was then being paid 11/1d a week, as a learner, for making 5,000 boxes an hour on the box machine. Later, new foreign machines arrived that would make 8,000 boxes an hour.

There were machines in the factory covered over with notices attached saying: 'These machines are idle through foreign competition.' She had never seen these rather antiquated machines working.

A general view of the match-making room. On the right: Mr Harry Moreland, with the works manager (Mr W.H. Rodway).

Staff fetching their free morning cup of tea and cake from the canteen trolley.

A Royal occasion at Moreland's during the Second World War; Queen Mary was photographed with members of the Moreland family during her visit to the factory on 14 October 1941.

Quite often groups of foreigners used to come round the works with the bosses – mostly Swedish, the staff thought.

The *Gloucester Journal* reported on 19 January 1925 that, after heavy flooding in Gloucester, Moreland's gave 10 tons of firewood to the Mayor's fund for drying out houses.

There was a break in the morning with a free cup of tea and a cake. Mr Harry came round one morning and remarked that the girls were taking too long with their break. His remedy was to have the cakes made smaller so they could be eaten quicker!

Discipline was strict at the factory. You had to stand when spoken to by the foreman and to obtain a job at the factory someone already there had to speak up for you.

Comments from other staff concerned the pleasant smell of Mr Harry's aftershave in comparison with the compo smell that clung to one's clothes (this was meant to be a compliment to his aftershave!). They also alluded to the fact that he wore drainpipe trousers!

Fires were plentiful and could be spectacular when thousands of matches in a machine went up. The mechanics who serviced and fixed the machines were, when an operator blew a machine whistle in the event of a fire, paid 2/6d for putting it out. The operator then had to go to the canteen for a glass of milk.

Mr Moulden first of all worked in the compo room laboratory and one day had his bicycle stolen. The police eventually recovered it, holding it as evidence. Moreland's noted his lateness and having heard the reason offered to buy him a new bike.

Another example of their generosity was concerning a mother and daughter who both worked at the factory. The daughter was knocked over one day by a lorry in the town and lost her leg. Moreland's later paid for a new artificial leg (there was no National Health Service in those days).

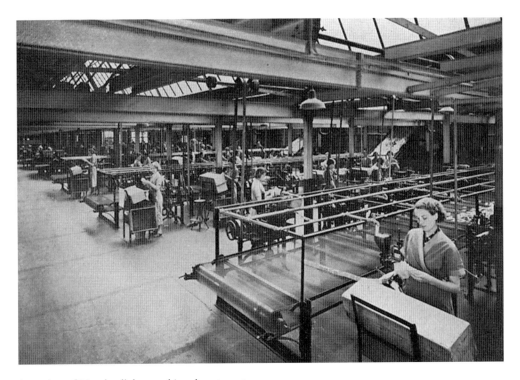

A portion of Moreland's box-making department.

Mr Moulden later became foreman of the Sanding and Packing Department and recalls that Customs & Excise had an office in the department. An officer used to sit there and count the cartons going past on the conveyor belt. The cartons were locked away in a cage at night. Excise duty had to be paid on every match manufactured.

Mr Ernest Brinkworth was the works production manager from 1936 until 1963 when he retired. He would arrive at the works on his bicycle at 6 a.m., later having breakfast there, and work until 6 p.m. When the works closed for holidays during the first two weeks of August, Mr Brinkworth would go in at times to keep an eye on the place and set the clocks.

In April 1941 the Standard Match factory was requisitioned by the government and all the machinery transferred to Moreland's, except for the sprinkler system. During the war the factory was used for the manufacture of aircraft fuel tanks.

After Queen Mary's visit in October the whole works had an extra 5/- in their pay packet for good behaviour!

Through the post, completely by surprise, came an exercise book from Mrs J. Sharpe of Gloucester with a wonderful account of the time when she left school and started work at Moreland's, which was her second job.

A promotional sticky label used for envelopes, etc.

A bundle of splints prior to being fed into the high-speed match machine.

I left school at fourteen, Easter time 1939.

I wanted to go dressmaking but Mavis Whiting got to the Bon Marché before me. So I had a job at Denton's, apprenticed making loose covers and curtains.

I had to wear hat and gloves. I turned up for work and the woman in charge was dressed all in black, thick black wool stockings, black dress with pin tucks, high collar and her grey hair pulled back into a tight bun, a spinster.

There was a large Old Moores Almanac on the wall which she studied every morning and said prayers.

Dora Major and I had a super job for a week. We had to put the sweets into the bottles for the toy sweet shops. We got sick of dolly mixture, but we did it faster than the others.

I had to work with a fat girl, Bessie. She used to sit on a three-legged stool, you couldn't see the stool. Her bum used to touch the floor.

Then Christmas came and I was out of work.

Mum took me down to Moreland's and waited outside for me. I went in and asked if there was any work.

The doorman, Harry Hodges, rang up and then took me to the lounge. I went into this big room with lots of armchairs and oil paintings on the walls, sat down and waited. The chairs smelt of leather. The door opened and an old gentleman walked in with a hard bowler hat on. I stood up as a young boy about my age and another man with a similar bowler hat walked in.

The old gentleman said he was Mr Moreland, the other said he was Mr Brinkworth (works manager) and the young man was Master Bob Moreland.

I was told to sit down and Mr Moreland asked why I wanted to work for him. I said I had heard such a lot about Moreland's. My mother had worked there, her sisters also worked there, in fact every one had worked for Moreland's at one time or another; also Great Grandad Manns had used barge boats for Moreland's timber.

I promised to work hard, to keep good time and I had to start work on 1 January 1940. I had to be measured for my overalls and a lady, who lived around the corner, came to measure me.

I was taken to the ladies room and met Miss Proctor and Miss Prosser and I was told how to behave. I didn't have to go out in curlers, not to go out without stockings as Mr Moreland's girls had to be neat and tidy at all times. I turned up for work and was given two brown overalls and was told that when I was sixteen I could have the colour of the room I worked in. I was told I would be in the packing room. We went up the iron stairs into a large room so long it seemed it would never end; the ceilings went up into the roof. I was handed over to Mr Lane who told me I would start by cleaning up and giving out.

I met a girl from school, Nellie Murcombe. We went around picking up the waste paper and putting it into a large deep bath-type container on wheels, then took it down in a lift you worked by hand to the fire hole.

Then we gave out glue. Well, the glue was made like giant Christmas puds. We had to cut it the best way we could; it was hard and sharp and tore our hands. The glue pots stood on large metal tables by the packing machines. They were heated pots – electric. We had shocks from them as well.

We were on the go all the time; sticking labels on wooden cases, stencilling the numbers and dates on them. Everyone wanted something. We also had nine machines to keep clear of gross packets.

I cried when I got home that night. My hands were all cut and had splinters from the wooden cases. My back and my legs ached. I begged my mum to let me leave and get another job, but all she said was 'Hard work won't kill you my girl. I had my share of hard work at Sammy's.'

So the days went by and I became one of Sammy's Angels.

Machines putting the striking sandpaper on England's Glory boxes. This picture was taken in 1927.

By working in the packing room we went to dinner at 11.30, back on the machines in the match making room for 12.30. They called it VPO, why I don't know.

I had to work a week for nothing – a week in hand really, but it was always said 'a week for nothing'. Well, pay day came and we all rushed down to collect it. We all lined up, some cracked jokes, some shouted 'Open the window, let's get paid.' So the hooter went, the windows opened and you shouted your number out. You were handed a tin 2in high and 1in wide with your money in it, all 8/5d. I was rich.

I took my pay home and my mum gave me a 1/- pocket money. Out of that I paid 8d for a pair of stockings from Marks & Spencer's and mum paid for the pictures once a week. She loved the pictures.

Moreland's hooter went every morning at 7am, again at 7.25 and lastly at 7.30. Everyone set their clocks by the hooter, it was heard all over Gloucester. I was late once and Mr Henry had to sign me in and I had a telling off.

Life went on and you got used to the aches and pains. You had to wait for someone to leave to have a machine yourself. If you were getting married you left. Mr Moreland didn't have married women at work, excepting widows; but he gave you a wedding present. You went to Mathew & Harris, the furniture shop and picked a dining table, four chairs, sideboard or a bedroom suite of wardrobe, dressing table and washstand.

If you got pregnant you could or would stay until you showed. Then Mr Moreland would come up and tell you himself that it was time you left and that, when it was over, your job would be waiting for you. I was with a girl like that when Mr Moreland came to her and told her, then shook hands. She came back after she had her baby and stopped until she married.

A sticky label used on envelopes.

I was moved over to the VPO and given a job on the DIP; that was the dipping process of the match. The splints, as they were called, came up from the splint room in the shape of a large penny, with two wires round them. They came up on a conveyor belt and you just reached up and took them off when you wanted them. They were punched into holes and this part of the machine was called Punchin In. This carried on all day while the splints went through a tank of paraffin wax.

The dip was a circle with a hole in the middle of the machine. The compo was in a little tank keeping warm and we turned the tap on every so often to keep the slab full of compo. The splints came down in batches and dipped into the compo on the slab. This is how the matches received their heads. They then went around the machine for two hours to dry.

It was my job to keep the tank clean and the compo running smooth. I also had to weigh samples of compo every two hours in grams.

At 3.30pm the Punchin In was disconnected and I had to clean up. The compo was scooped up off the slab and the gate and bars put into a flat tank of boiling water and I cleaned the hand compo off. We used to use large hooks to fish the things out of the tank for scrubbing.

The floors had to be spotless. The Governor, Mr Moreland, wouldn't have a match or a spot of oil on the floor; so, on Fridays I had a little bucket of paraffin and I would wash all around the machine on my hands and knees.

Sometimes I had to go on 'passing'. That was another part of the machine – picking off broken matches before the boxes closed. Another part of the huge machine, situated upstairs, was called a 'Ruffler'. The boxes were blown over from the box room through large metal pipes, called 'Ducks', into skips; the drawers and cases coming separately. They went down chutes onto the machine below to fill up with matches. The boxes then went back to the sanding machines for a little bit of sandpaper to be stuck on them. They had to be fed into the machine a certain way otherwise you had a white end showing where the sandpaper ought to be.

We had a bonus at the end of the month which was given out in the kitchen at the top of the building. Here we could boil a kettle for tea, and cook our own food if unable to go home to dinner, as we didn't have a canteen at the time.

(A) Sticker on the back of a box wishing Princess Elizabeth and the Duke of Edinburgh best wishes for their married life, and their visit in 1947 is remembered. Edinburgh, however, is spelt wrongly. (B) 1890s sulphur matches. (C) England's Glory label 1905–10.

The Governor used to stand by a table and hand out the bonus. Mr Pritchard and Mr Brinkworth told the Governor our names as we received the bonus, thanked him and promised to work harder next month.

Most of the girls used the money on clothes or hair dos as 'Sammy's Girls' were smart and well groomed.

The war was on, the blackouts went up, lights were dimmed and some of the girls left. They were offered more money to work elsewhere. I too left but I also went back later and saw Moreland's change.

The girls now wore turbans over their curls, no stockings. They didn't have the same pride as we did. The machines were speeded up and departments closed down. The veneer room disappeared and we had cardboard skillets now. With cartons to put the matches in, the wooden crates went. The printing room was made smaller and the Diamond Room, which housed the match making machines my mother worked on, went. The splints now came in boxes from Canada.

Moreland's is no more but I will never forget the smell of the compo; smoke will always bring back memories of the smell of a fire on the match machines, the smell of the paste-making machine. Oh, so many smells! The jokes are even gone from the boxes.

I was fifteen when I started and a married woman when I left.

Moreland's was a family firm – who would have ever dreamt it could close?

The Governor came in an electric car and Mr Bobby rode his bike. We used to race each other down Stroud Road.

Mr Sam came out of the forces and went into the firm and Mr Harry to Simmon Barron's. Mr Henry went to live at Highnam. Miss Jane got married and we all turned up to her wedding. April gave her a spoon and we all smothered everyone with confetti. Mr Henry came and thanked me for making her day.

Auntie Nell worked in the box room with me and Auntie Ann (Merrett). Grannie Mann's sister also worked with us. Two girls rode their bikes in from Newent, others from Moreton Valance and Brockworth, for years in all weathers, just to work at Moreland's.

Getting a place at Moreland's was like getting one at Harrods, you had to be recommended. I got many people work there and we were well looked after having a morning tea break with cake, biscuits and bread roll, etc. There was half pay if sick to be collected from the welfare office; hospital treatment was also paid for if you couldn't afford it – many went to London for treatment. Half a load of logs and free uniforms – it was one big family. Whole families worked there: the Gallings, Billinghams, Jones, Evans, Kemmits, Bicks and Coles for some.

I eventually left and went nursing and met Mr Bob several times when on nursing homes, he's still the same.

I am retired now and spend my time sewing, knitting, doll making and have my little dogs to love.

You will never find a family firm again like Moreland's.

I was proud to be one of Sammy's Angels.

Thank you, Mrs Sharpe, for that gem.

The Second World War gave more notice of its coming and the industry was far better prepared than on the previous occasion. Forty-five employees went off to the Armed Services and the factory continued to keep production at its highest under difficult circumstances. It also made striker sticks for bombs and completed finishing work on waterproof match containers.

At the request of the Government, a proportion of the Moreland's boxes carried war effort slogans, such as 'Save Fuel for Battle', in the space normally occupied by the jokes.

Mrs Jones remembers, during the war, a bomb falling in Gloucester while two girls were walking to work. One ran on ahead whilst the other hid under a bush. She later complained that she had been left on her own. Both whispered for some time afterwards in case the planes could hear them!

For the visit of the Queen and Prince Philip to the factory on 3 May 1955 and later for the banquet at the Guildhall special boxes of matches were made and placed on the banquet table. Lena Turk made all these by hand.

The labels were counted out to her and any spoiled had to be handed back, so each label and box were accounted for.

In 1961, having joined the company in 1913 and been a board member since 1920, Henry retired and left his two sons Samuel and Robert to run the business as managing director and works director, respectively.

JOIN YOUR
COUNTY YEOMANRY
REGIMENT

THE
ROYAL
GLOUCESTERSHIRE
HUSSARS

BRITISH MATCHES

AVERAGE CONTENTS 46

seven
The Labels

its of the Best Quality.
J. HOFF
Rock Hotel,
WESTHAM,
WEYMOUTH.

Moreland's

Try the
"CALEDONIAN"

NRY V. WALTERS
acconist,
107, Southgate St.,
LOUCESTER.

How the first labels for SJM's boxes of matches were printed is not known – but they were probably done by a local printer. Certainly the factory was printing its own labels well before 1900 and appears to have always printed its own with a few exceptions. Which the exceptions were is not known but records show that Martin Billington, Son & Co., of Livery Street, Birmingham, and James Upton, Cambridge Street, also of Birmingham, both printers, were used by Moreland's at times. Whether this was for labels or other material is unclear.

H.R. Clarke of Bristol printed labels for Octavius Hunt of Bristol and for the Crown Match Works of Cardiff. There is one label, however, with the Moreland name and that of the printer H.R. Clarke on the same label, which poses a few questions. Were there any other labels Clarke printed for Moreland that did not have the Moreland name attached? As it has not generally been appreciated that Clarke printed labels for Moreland, but mostly only for the Hunt and Crown factories, are any of the labels that are attributed to Octavius Hunt actually Moreland brands? No doubt as other labels turn up some of these questions may be answered.

The two main types of labels are known as singles (pasted onto one side of the box) and ARTBs. This type of label goes 'All Round The Box' – hence its name. The older labels sometimes covered the front and back and one side, with the striking surface not actually part

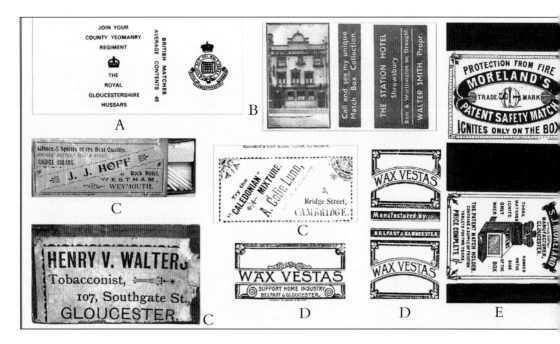

(A) Label of the Royal Gloucestershire Hussars, TA Regiment (of which the author was a member from 1959 to 1960) was issued in 1966, but the Regiment closed down in 1967 except for a small unit at Cirencester, Glos. (B) These labels appear in two colours, black and a sepia rust-brown on white. They were made for Mr Walter Smith, proprietor of the Station Hotel, Shrewsbury in the mid- to late 1920s. There are no flaps on the labels as they were stuck onto Moreland boxes after manufacture to allow the striking surface to be exposed. Mr Smith collected complete boxes with some 8,000 items and allowed visitors to take a box and make a contribution to St Dunstan's. (C) The two boxes and the Lunn label are about 1900 or earlier. (D) The two Wax Vestas labels were possibly samples and not circulated. The Moreland name in the blank spaces has not reproduced. This association came about because of a great friendship between the family and Bertie Maguire. (E) A fine early label of the 1870s, black on buff paper. All labels are shown here at half actual size.

of the label. Whilst most ARTBs covered all four surfaces, the majority had tabs that overlapped each other on the fourth side with the striking surface on top.

It is unfortunate that in many older collections labels were customarily cut with just the two main panels being kept. This practice has ruined so many wonderful examples of Victorian and Edwardian engraving and has at the same time also vastly reduced the value of such labels. While a few collectors will not keep an incomplete label, others feel that something is better than nothing – hoping that a complete or fuller example will turn up one day.

The older boxes were made of a wooden veneer, partly scored through in the correct place so as to bend and fold it over to make the outer box. The label was then glued over this box. The inner trays were, for some time, also made from veneer until the use of card began around the time of the First World War.

Skillets were another type of matchbox, being made completely from cardboard with the design printed directly onto the card. They were first introduced around 1900 and eventually took over UK production in the 1960s and 70s.

Some collectors save only labels, some only boxes and others both. Labels do take up less space and skillets are sometimes carefully taken apart and then flattened. Some people thin them. This is done by splitting the card on the reverse of the printed side and, with skill, can reduce the skillet by two thirds in thickness. It is argued by some that the skillet is then spoilt. One may agree or say that they are almost worthless in any case and so it does not matter. But in a hundred years' time people may look at things differently. Look what happened to Edwardian collections of labels that were trimmed with scissors. It was the fashion and obviously did not matter at the time. Now it is regretted!

Boxes made from plastic appeared in the 1970s and 80s but never seemed to catch on.

A good old box in fine condition, especially when it still has its contents, does look very fetching when making up a display for an exhibition. Sadly all these items need to be stored out of the light to prevent fading and often are very brittle, needing careful handling.

During the time that Moreland's produced matches, many different brand names emerged and also many variations of the same label. This book is not a record of all the different variations produced but instead tries to show the different brands of labels. No doubt some will argue that I have left out many labels that might be similar to the ones shown but are different enough to justify

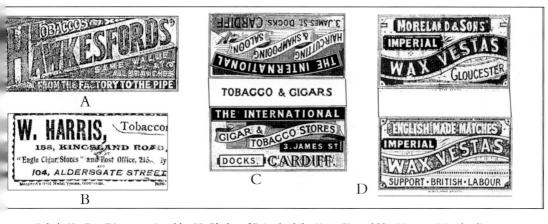

Labels (A, C & D) were printed by H. Clarke of Bristol whilst (A & C) could be Hunt or Moreland? (D) is the only label I have seen printed by Clarke that is a Moreland brand. These two panels are cut and probably go together. (B) is red on buff *c*.1897–1900. All labels are shown here at half actual size.

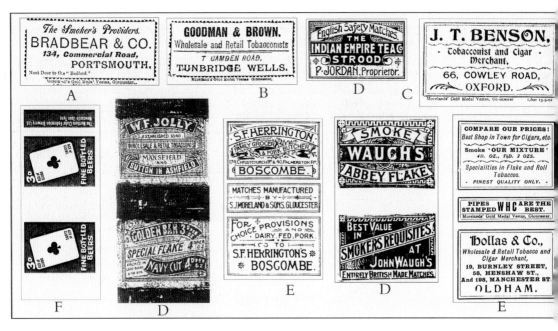

Above: (A, B & D) are black on buff. (A) All c.1897–1905. (C & E) Thought to be Moreland by R. W-H and D. v. der P. It is possible W. Jolly could be Belgian. (C) Brick red on off-white or magenta on buff. (D & E) Two labels of c.1897–1910. (F) The oddity in this illustration: a green, black on white label of several versions produced in the later 1960s–1972. All labels are shown here at half actual size.

Below: (A) This example was produced from a printing block found at the factory by Bob Moreland. A similar style label was produced by Standard Match and also a skillet by Midland Match. Label (B) was printed in 1900 with handwriting of Harry Moreland, managing director. (C) 'As Used by Conn' was a cartoon used on the label of 'British Matches', 'Use Moreland Matches' and 'The Shaughraun'. This latter label dates from the second half of the 1870s. There is also a similar label entitled 'Gloucester Match' instead of Moreland on the centre panel. The Shaughraun was the name of a theatrical production, a play that opened in London during September 1875. The scene, seven years earlier, was set in County Sligo on the west coast of Ireland. Boucicault, its author, played Conn the title character, the shaughraun or vagabond (in Irish 'seachran' means wandering). He roamed with his dog and peaked cap as far as Australia in search of his heart-wish. The label (D) was the only label registered by Gloucester Match Co., Bristol Road, Gloucester on 9 March 1911. All labels are shown here at half actual size.

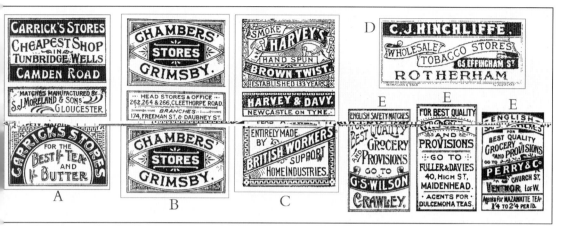

(A) Black on buff, c.1900. (B) In the style of early 1900s Moreland. (C) Magenta on buff and thought to be Moreland. (D) Red and dark blue on buff. (E) Possibly back labels to Moreland boxes c.1898–1900 according to D. v der P. Also included in this series of labels are W. Figgins, Devises; Older Bros, Emsworth; and Benett Bros of Bognor. All labels are shown here at half actual size.

reproducing them. I would say in answer, that is the purpose of a catalogue, which this book is not. If you feel this way then please start a catalogue and I will do all I can to help. It is needed!

If you are reading this book as a collector or a potential collector there is plenty of scope, even though Moreland's has been gone for nearly thirty years now. Pre-1900 labels and boxes are difficult to obtain and expensive. Many labels or boxes from before the Second World War are readily obtainable for less than £5 each while post-war skillets can be had for two or three pence each. Perhaps the England's Glory labels or skillets appeal to you? In total there were about 18,000 different ones produced – so I am told. (Derek Saunders produced two excellent catalogues of England's Glory covering 1891–1972.) I am sure there are still many interesting discoveries to be made whilst collecting Moreland labels, as new items are still surfacing in the form of labels and whole boxes.

There are some labels shown in monochrome that cannot be definitely attributed to Moreland. In the colour section the same applies to Old Tom, Robert Sinclairs and Reese & Gwillim. I have included them mainly because they were listed as probably Moreland by the late David van der Plank and Raymond Wheatley-Hubbard who both had wonderful British collections and a lot of knowledge.

The Workman's is another uncertain brand that was printed by H.R. Clark and was also a brand produced by Octavius Hunt in a different design and colour to the one shown. It is thought by some that this particular version may well be by Moreland.

I find these advertising and customer labels very interesting, probably because they are around a hundred years old now and give us some insight into the important items of those days. As I am finishing writing this, only two weeks away from completion, I have just acquired another customer label from around 1900, which nearly did not make these records.

I notice in a catalogue of Clutterbuck & Griffin, dated June 1871, that they were selling Moreland's Safetys, Damp Proofs, Paraffins & Ruby. (One still to find?)

The following information was given to me by Moreland employees:
Scottish Bluebell were produced at Gloucester from about 1954, Harlequin Matches from 1962/63 and were still produced in 1972. Bo-Peep were made for Maguire & Patterson for

a while. Others made were: Lucky Strike, Standard, Lutona and various Variety and Souvenir presentation packs of birds, tartans, flowers, etc. as well as Cook's Matches, Winfield – trade mark of Woolworths, also Co-op and Swan matches (until closure). Hotspur and Light Brigade were made for Midland Match during the war and packed in special cases.

The following illustrations are taken from the Registered Trade Marks. Many names or designs were registered hopefully to stop others stealing the idea. It did not always work and there have been some instances of legal action to prevent use by a third party.

The part of the colour section showing later labels from the 1950s onwards, particularly after 1972 when the factory assumed branch status, is almost certainly not a full record of the labels produced. Most of them were 'customer' labels, Swan being one exception, and tend to be out of my collecting interest and knowledge.

During this period, only skillets were produced – that is, the label was printed directly onto a cardboard outer without a paper label. (One good point about skillet collecting in general is that they have mostly been recorded in various excellent publications by D. Millen and R. Tolson, so you actually know what was produced.)

The following are some examples taken from *The Trades Mark Journal*:

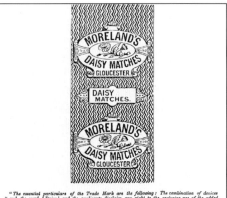

"*The essential particulars of the Trade Mark are the following : The combination of devices and the word 'Daisy,' and the applicants disclaim any right to the exclusive use of the added matter, except in so far as it consists of their own name.*"

235,251. Matches. S. J. MORELAND AND SONS, Bristol Road, Gloucester, Gloucestershire ; Timber Importers and Match Manufacturers.—5th January 1901.

137,209. Matches. S. J. MORELAND & SONS, Bristol Road, Gloucester, Gloucestershire ; Match Manufacturers.—27th October 1911. The applicants and their predecessors in business have used the said Mark within the United Kingdom in respect of the said Goods continuously since five years before the 13th August 1875. (*To be associated. Sect. 24.*)

335,911. Matches. S. J. Moreland and Sons, Bristol Road, Gloucester, Gloucestershire; Timber Importers and Match Manufacturers.—29th August 1911.

158,168. Matches. S. J. Moreland & Sons, Gloucester; Timber Importers.—14th August 1891. Mark used by applicants and predecessors in business about five years before the 13th August 1875.

393,017. Matches. S. J. Moreland and Sons, Limited, Bristol Road, Gloucester; Match Manufacturers.—4th July 1919. (*To be associated. Sect. 24.*)

" *The essential particular of the Trade Mark is the device, and the applicants disclaim any right to* " *the exclusive use of the added matter, except in so far as it consists of their own name.*"

221,985. Matches. S. J. Moreland & Sons, Bristol Road, Gloucester, Gloucestershire; Timber Importers.—5th April 1899.

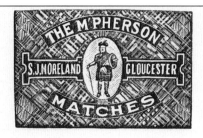

User claimed from 31st December, 1870.

B425,092. Matches. S. J. MORELAND & SONS, LIMITED, Bristol Road Match Factory, Bristol Road, Gloucester, Gloucestershire ; Timber Importers.—7th April, 1922.

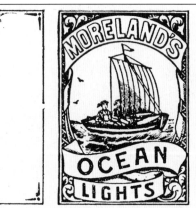

308,969. Matches. S. J. MORELAND AND SONS, Bristol Road, Gloucester, Gloucesters Timber Importers and Match Manufacturers.—18th December 1908. The applicants and predecessors in business have used the said Trade Mark in respect of the said Goods continuously two years before the 13th August 1875. (*To be associated. Sect. 24.*)

No claim is made to the exclusive use of the word " Moreland's."

405,981. Matches included in Class 47. S. J. MORELAND AND SONS, LIMITED, Bristol Roa Gloucester ; Match Manufacturers.—12th July 1920. (*To be associated Sect. 24.*)

USE

England's Glory

MATCHES

MORELAND

GLOUCESTER

eight

Hardware and Advertising

Advertising items produced by match companies are known as hardware to the collector. Bryant & May were the largest producers, followed by Moreland, mainly because both companies lasted longer than their competitors. This was partly due to the fact that Bryant & May bought out much of the opposition, quite often closing them down soon afterwards.

Collectors of match items can collect labels, boxes, and hardware as well as general match containers and holders, or perhaps they might focus on just one of these and maybe from just one company. We are all different and there is so much scope. Hardware, in different forms, can quite often be found at antique fairs, flea markets and car boot sales. You never know your luck. If you find something interesting – haggle, do not automatically pay the asking price. If the price is too high – unless it is something exceptional – walk away, there will be another opportunity. I have done this several times on rarer items and regretted it!

In this chapter I am trying to give a feel for the hardware put out by Moreland's for advertising purposes.

Some items are just useful – such as pencils and tins for vesta matches, whilst the range goes from a water jug, playing cards and crib boards to ashtrays, to give but a few examples.

Left: A pack of spills from the 1880s.

Below: A box of toothpicks, probably 1880s.

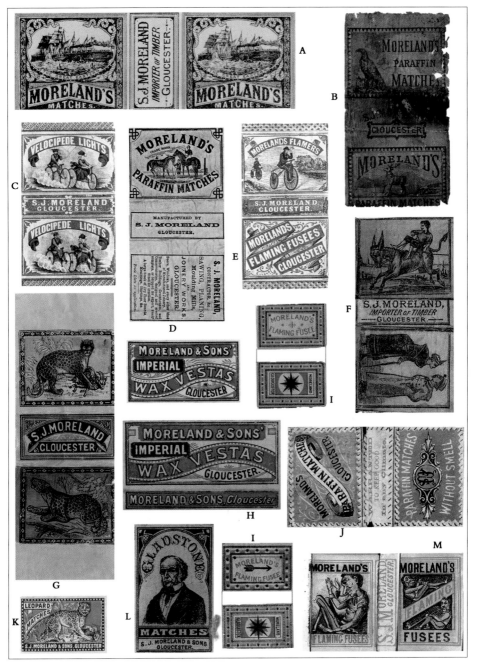

1 (A) Wonderful early label *c.*1870. (B) Probably late 1870s. (C & E) A lovely pair of labels 1870–80. (D) One of the earliest labels from 1867. (F) Early 1870s – copied from a complete box. (G) One of several similar labels *c.*1880. (H) Two of several different versions of Imperial Wax Vestas. (I) Two small-cut ARTBs, known as waistcoat pocket size. (J) Early 1870s – very similar to the Belcher, Gee label of 1871. (K) Another pre-1900 Leopard-cut label. (L) 1880s/1890s, probably to mark Gladstone's third or fourth return as Prime Minister. (M) *c.*1871 – copied from a box that contains wonderful large-headed matches on each end of the stick.

2 (A) Single label in use in 1895, also in orange and black on bright yellow. (B) The original Arctic label 1895 when Franklin perished in the North West Passage. (C) Cut ARTB Safety Matches from *c.*1900.
(D) Braided Stars form late 1870s. (F) Pre-1913 single label. (E & G) Two good labels c.1880.
(H) Wolverhampton FC, list of the season's fixtures for 1898 – believed to be a Moreland label. (I) Skipper *c.*1900 – also in purple and also made by Gloucester Match. (J) Old England For Ever 1900 – said to be copied from an oil painting in the boardroom. (K) Handsome label of 1880–1900, also in red, black on buff and in different sizes. (L) Tally Ho is pre-1900, the larger one may be a packet label, the smaller one also in red, blue on buff as ARTB. (M) Cut ARTB, probably 1890s. All labels are shown here at 40 per cent actual size.

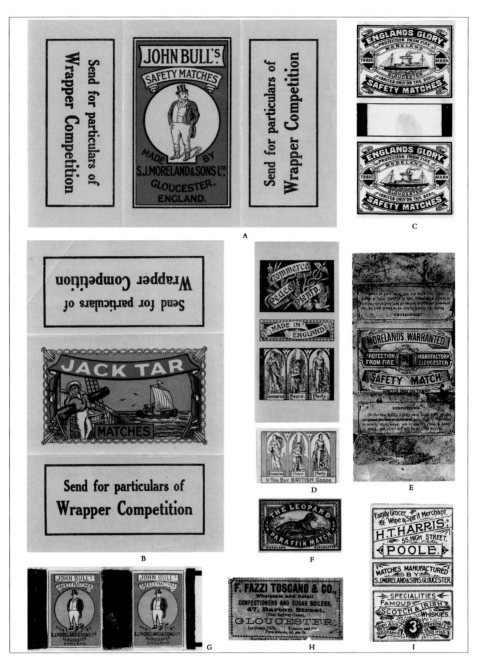

3 (A) Also with blue in the circle, and (B) are two glazed wrappers maybe around 1920 or earlier. (C) England's Glory label of 1899–1900 but may have not been issued and could be a printer's pull. (D) Issued 1911. (E) A fine label *c*.1870. (F) Single label – one of several designs. (G) *c*.1912 – first registered 1900. (H) Lovely local label *c*.1895–1905. (I) Early 1900s. All labels are shown here at 40 per cent actual size.

4 (A) Another Leopard ARTB, also as a single. (B) Two 1930–40 versions of Jack Tar, which was registered in 1919. (C) A lovely box of Wax Vestas dated 1904. (D) 1920–30, one of many different Leek Matches made for the Welsh market, first registered in 1899. (E & F) 1920–30s generally accepted as Moreland. (G & J) Said by R. W-H and D. v der P. to be Moreland, (J) is believed to go together as shown. (H) Assumed to be both Moreland, early 1900s. (I) Labels with sticky backs to go on boxes as required by the Government during the Second World War. (K) Customer label made for Charles Dickens of Cheltenham, registered 14 September 1925. All labels are shown here at 40 per cent actual size.

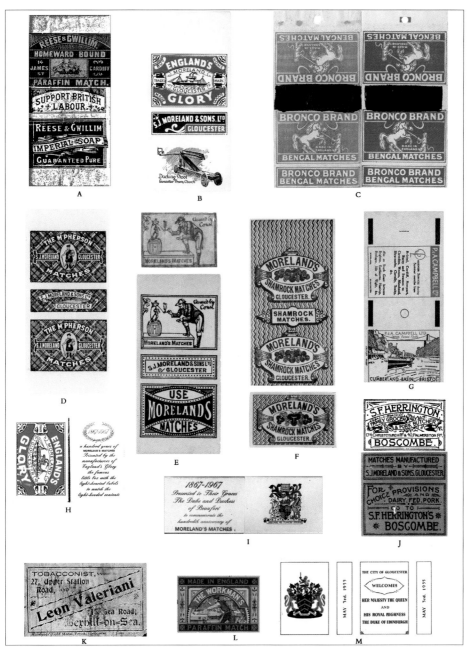

5 (A) Thought to be Moreland. (B) Ducking Stool at Leominster Priory Church issued 1921–22. (C) Two skillets made by Moreland for Octavius Hunt around 1970? Bronco registered by Hunt in 1924. (D) Registered in 1922 but first issued in 1870. (E) 1911–1920s. (F) Similar in design to Daisy, which was registered in 1901 but never used. (G) One of two similar labels issued in the 1930s. (H & I) Front and back views of two centenary boxes. (J) Rare customer label of early 1900s. (K) *c*.1897–1905. (L) A label, printed by Clarke of Bristol, with same name and similarities to the O. Hunt label. (M) Label issued to commemorate visit by the Queen and Prince Philip in 1955. All labels are shown here at 40 per cent actual size.

6 Some of the post-war labels or skillets made at Gloucester mostly for different customers. The Brymay box, shown here at full size, was the last skillet to come off No.2 machine, which closed down, never to be run again, at 4.15 p.m. on 29 January 1972. All other labels are 40 per cent actual size.

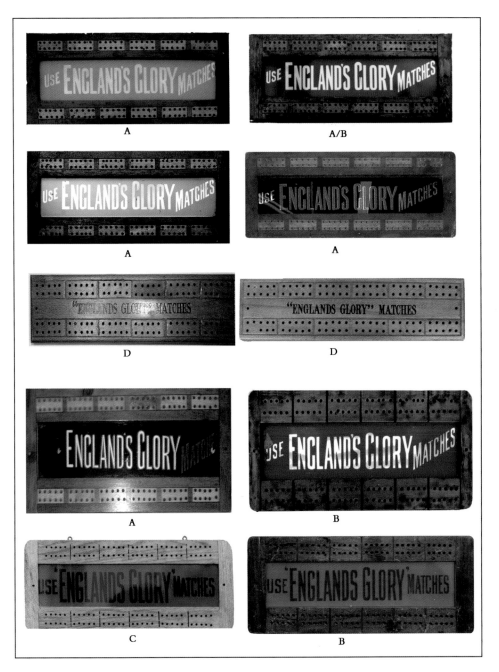

7 A selection of crib boards. (A) Pattern is *c*.1910–20. (B) Also comes with rounded corners *c*.1920s. (C) 1930s and comes with and without glass. (D) Pattern is 1950s.

8 Various different Moreland ashtrays. (A) Concorde 1969. (B) Glass 1910–20. It is suggested that the coloured one is not original. (C) Copper ashtray. (D) Late 1920s. (E) *c.*1950. (F) Above: The Spread Eagle, Witham, Essex, made by Grays Potteries & Causton of London; below: The Woodman at Highgate (now rebuilt) made by Causton. (H) Bakerlite 1930s. (G) Unusual 1950s(?) England's Glory ashtray.

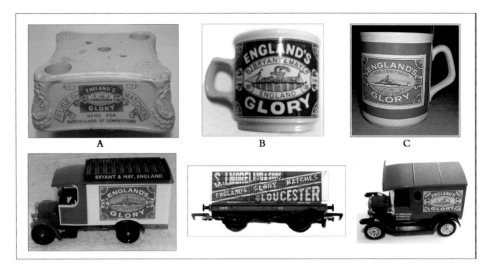

9 Post-war advertising items. (A) Porcelain stand made for a bell 1920s. Note in (B) and (C) the name Moreland has been dropped – late 1970s.

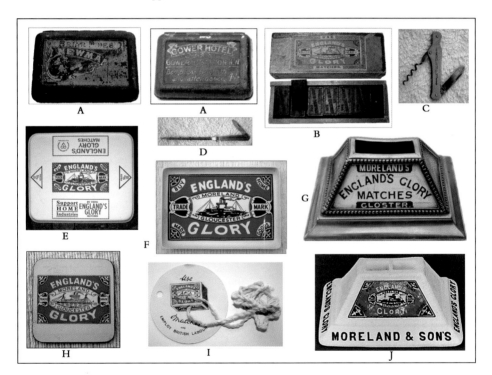

10 (A) Wax Vesta tins c.1900 – stamped Moreland; there is also an EG tin but the picture is of too poor a quality to show. (B) Set of dominoes in box c.1905. (C) Penknife and corkscrew.
(D) Penknife and letter opener. (E) Melamine tray 1972. (F) 1960s ashtray. (G) Bar match holder, design registered in 1892, made by Jenkinson of Birmingham. (H) Melamine 1960–70s coaster.
(I) Whizzer game c.1930s. Card with a string when pulled between hands correctly would revolve, hum and rewind itself. (J) Another bar match holder in porcelain.

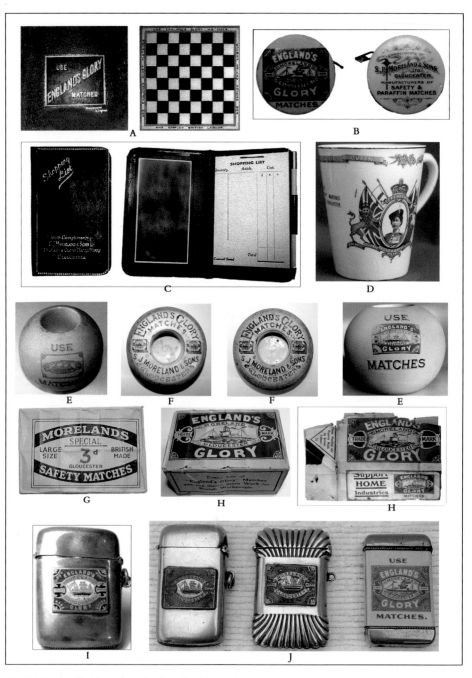

11 (A) England's Glory draughts board sold on ebay in 2004. (B) Front and back of 1920s sewing tape measure. (C) Delightful case with shopping list and mirror. (D) E II R coronation mug stamped 'Use England's Glory Matches, Morelands Ltd, Gloucester'. (E) Two England's Glory match pots. (F) Two different ones of several similar match tyres, 1910–20. (G) Dozen pack of Safety Matches late 1960s. (H) Two wartime dozen wrappers. (I) Silver and enamelled Vesta case, Birmingham 1904, courtesy of Gloucester City Council. (J) Three examples of several different Vesta cases of early 1900s.

12 (A) Jacket lapel badge for Wembley Exhibition 1924. (B) Tea cosy late 1960s–early 1970s. (C) Plastic match game. (D) Late 1960s apron. (E) Wax Vesta tin – photo courtesy of Gloucester City Council. (F) Oven cloth late 1970s.

13 (A) One of several different coloured plastic boxes for Harlequin matches. (B) Brass and glass coaster, 11.5cm diameter – 1920s. (C) Painted tin pub tray 32cm diameter. (D) Shop change mat. (E) Tin enamelled sign, c.1910, about 60cm square. (F) Moreland's Matches glass match holder. (G) Delightful model of boat made for matchbox. (H) Pen and pencil set – 1967. (I) Porcelain framed advert for shop. (J) Pre-war engraved water jug.

14 6ft tall cut-out figures used for touring agricultural shows and exhibitions before the Second World War to promote Moreland's products. Photographed courtesy of Robert Opie in the Packaging Museum storeroom.

15 (A) Two pub trays 31cm in diameter. (B) Picture of boxers, enamelled on tin, early 1900s.

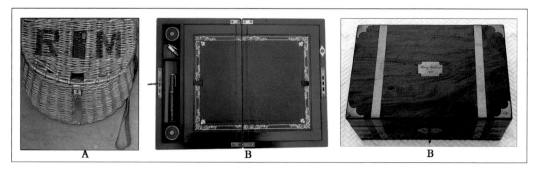

16 (A) Fishing basket that once belonged to Robert Moreland. (B) This Victorian walnut writing slope is inscribed on the brass plate 'Harry Moreland 1907'. Working in the joinery unit opposite mine was an elderly chap, who on hearing I was writing a book on Moreland's, said he had a box belonging to the family to which his wife was related. Eventually he produced this writing slope, which I purchased.

17 Below: This rare, impressed, coloured card advertising poster – by Barclay & Fry, colour printers of London – was issued by Moreland's *c.*1900–1910 to promote their sales. The design was based on a picture issued in the 1870s of HMS *Devastation*. She was a twin-screw, iron-turret battleship, launched at HM Dockyard, Portsmouth in 1871 and completed in 1873. 285ft long, with a beam of 62ft, she displaced 9,188 tons and her 5,600hp engines gave her a speed of 13 knots. She carried four 35-ton guns and a complement of 250 men. Her armour plating was 10 to 12in thick and her total armour weighed 2,224 tons. Her first captain was Fred Richards. In 1879 she was one of the first vessels to be fitted with electric light, and Wild's Electro Magnetic Lighting Apparatus was used. She was taken out of service in 1908.

18 Right: (A) Four different pre-war travellers' samples. (B) Traveller's card. (C) Shop wall hook for paper bags. (D) Plastic wall box holder saying 'Take one not the box'. (E) Factory mock up of box. (F) Shop door 'Open/Closed' sign. (G) Painted chipboard sign. (H) Four shop match dispensers.

THE JOKER

19 A selection of various playing cards produced over the years.

A

B

C

D

E

E

F

H

I

J

G

20 (A) 1950s, (B) c.1965 and (C) are thick card mounts for shop advertising. (D) Book of prizes for wrappers. (E) Two paper adverts for display. (F) Safety Match carrier bag. (G) Safety Match pencil. (H) Club score card. (I) Selection of headed stationery. (J) Selection of company envelopes.

■ Striking collection – Marcus Moore takes a last look at the 5,000 England's Glory matchboxes he has pasted on the walls of his stairway.   Photos: Paul Nicholls

They're Adam's Glory!

ADAM Horovitz is determined to ensure his next-door neighbour's bizarre tradition is not going, going, gone.

For the 29-year-old of Horns Road in Stroud is now the proud owner of 5,071 England's Glory matchboxes – painstakingly collected by theatre director and BBC scriptwriter Marcus Moore over the past 15 years.

Adam fought off ferocious competition from some 12 fellow bidders at an auction held in Marcus's house yesterday.

Friends, neighbours and even one avid matchbox collector from Luton gathered for the auction.

But Adam's £75.50p bid brought the hammer down and thousands of colourful little boxes were his.

Determined to follow in the footsteps of his close friend, Adam intends to stick every one of the matchboxes – formerly made at the Moreland's factory in Bristol Road, Gloucester – on his hall and stairway wall.

"I have already stuck three of the boxes onto the wall with brown tape and now intend to have a bath to contemplate my achievement," he said.

Former teacher Marcus was faced with a dilemma when he decided to move to Cirencester – he didn't know what to do with his collection.

"I found an answer which suited my fondness for fun and decided to sell the collection by auction, with the proceeds going to charity," he said.

The money will go towards cancer research and reafforestation charities.

■ Some of the collection of matchboxes, dating back to the 1960s. Left: The crowd gathers for the auction.

21 A fairly recent cutting from a local newspaper shows Marcus Moore demonstrating a somewhat bizarre system of storing his collection of 5,000 plus England's Glory skillets.

Many items were provided for shops to display and invite or persuade customers to purchase Moreland products, so most are aimed at England's Glory.

Rather than list them it seems more interesting to show pictures, but these will only be a representation and will not show small differences between similar items.

A nearly full box of England's Glory pencils.

Front and inside of an advertising paper wallet for holding safety pins.

Above: Wooden proof printing block for John Bull, *c.*1900.

Left: A moulded pint beer mug.

The majority of Moreland hardware is interesting and of good quality. In general terms, items nearer the end of the factory's life tend to be less desirable. Later items were marked as Bryant & May instead of Moreland, which I have tended not to collect.

Some smaller articles of everyday life like razor blade holders, the box of pencils and the safety pin holder, are little gems and make a colourful display.

Many items are still turning up that only seem to exist in ones or twos. The world, out there, is a collector's paradise!

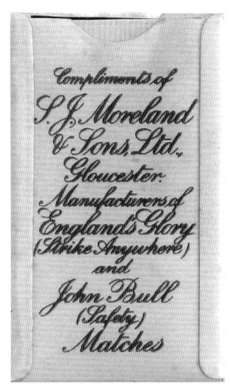

Above: Front and back of one of two razor-blade packets advertising England's Glory.

Right: A 1960s plastic paperweight.

'Working for Bryant & May'
– issued in the mid-1960s.

Below left: A very unusual
early glass paperweight, which
unfortunately had been used as a
hammer and damaged.

Below right: Another different
porcelain tyre match holder.

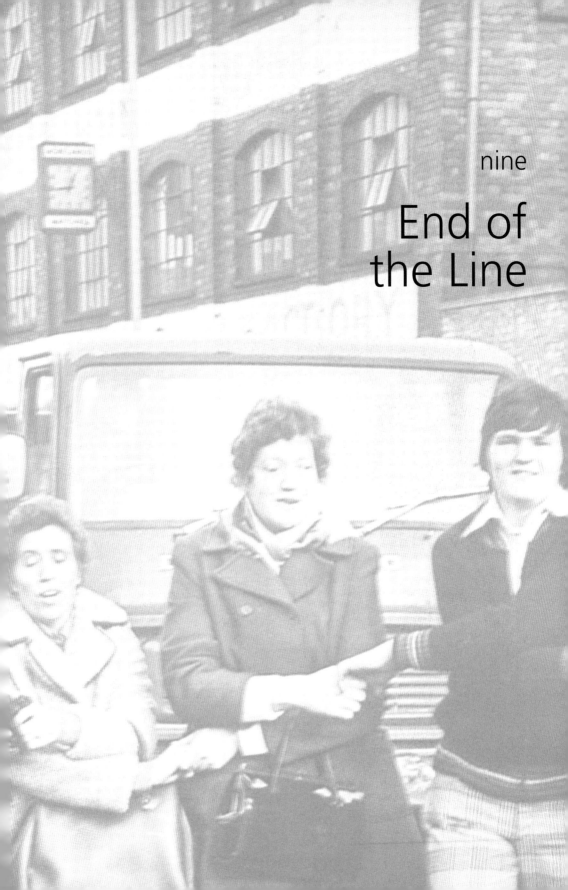

nine

End of
the Line

Match making in the 1960s was a highly mechanised operation, essential to maintain the enormous output of 50 million matches each working day.

A surprising number of components were used in the process: wood, obviously, mostly poplar from Canada, cardboard and paper and several different chemicals and ingredients. Amongst them were chlorate of potash, sulphur, phosphorus, zinc oxide, paraffin wax, glue, glass and plaster of Paris. The safety match heads contained chlorate of potash and sulphur, which ignites immediately contact is made with red phosphorus on the striking surface of the matchbox. 'Strike anywhere' heads have a mixture of chlorate of potash and sesquisulphide of phosphorus. Many of these chemicals were supplied by Albright & Wilson of Oldbury, near Birmingham, who were the main chemical suppliers to the match industry from about 1860. They produced the first amorphous phosphorous in 1862, enabling safety matches to be manufactured.

Roy Wood started at Moreland's in the early 1940s, spending the last fifteen years as foreman of the New Mill, and shared some of his memories of his working days. He recalled that:

Any commemorative days celebrated at the factory were always done properly and in style. The council yard at the rear was taken over, which used to be the refuse depot when horse-drawn vehicles were in use. A large marquee, complete with heating, would be erected and all the company employees, past and present, as well as the mayor, etc. would all be invited.

At the Queen's coronation everyone was given a beaker with Moreland's name added. [These seem to be very scarce nowadays].

Pay in 1946 was £4 a week with the hours of 7.30am–5.30pm and 7.30am–12.30pm on Saturdays.

At Christmas a married foreman received, as an extra, an enormous turkey and his wife would be given a box of chocolates.

Moreland's also used to buy in fireworks from Octavius Hunt to sell on to the employees for 5 November. The majority of splints were imported from the mid-1950s and arrived in large wired bundles.

West Country sales were conducted from the Exeter depot which opened about 1957. The staff consisted of a manager, sales rep and driver. The main sales in the West Country were Moreland's Safeties and England's Glory and any special labels such as the Mayflower and Nonsuch. Customer labels went mostly to the Midlands whilst strongholds of England's Glory were Bristol, South Wales and the Midlands. Bryant & May amalgamated the sales force with theirs in 1970.

On 13 August 1958 Charles Shadgett and John Ireland retired, having completed 100 years of service at the factory between them. John Ireland earned seven shillings a week when he started there fifty-three years previously. Building began in 1964 on a new splint room at a cost of £50,000, which was to be ready the following year. It was constructed on part of the yard in Seymour Road, purchased from the council. Logs would enter one end of the building and leave the other end as splints.

The canteen accounts for the half-year in 1967 reported a loss of £3,568, which included a profit of £59 on the sale of sweets. (*Gloucester dentists did well!*)

In 1971 it was minuted that the floor stocks were in a muddle due to pressure of work – overtime was then being worked on two evenings a week and extra time on Friday afternoons. The pressure was due to the destruction of the Belfast factory and a sudden order from Wills Tobacco for 20,000 gross in 'Souvenir' style. In September it was recommended to erect a two-storey extension to the Stroud Road end of the match room at a cost of £60,000. A new printing room was underway at £25,000 and also the strengthening of the match room floor for the Swan machines. That year an order was also placed for England's Glory tea cosies.

Bryant & May reduced the factory to branch status in 1972 when Sam Moreland retired. On 13 April 1972 it was decided to liquidate S.J. Moreland & Sond Ltd, as S.J. Moreland & Sons (Holdings) Ltd had been formed in 1966, and offers were being sought for the purchase of Hempstead Wharf.

From the point of view of those working on the factory floor it must have seemed a sudden decision to close the works in 1976. A new compo room had just been built a year previously and the council yard was due to be built on for a factory extension with a new entrance and gates.

Speculation at the works suspected that, as the demand for matches was dwindling, one factory had to go. Perhaps Liverpool had managed to obtain grants for improvements but not Gloucester?

An article in the Economist published on 18 October 1975 stated:

Matches
Sweden's Glory
Britain's five self-styled match merchants (entrepreneurial family firms to a man) have joined forces with the latest would-be worker's co-operative to do battle with the giants of the international match business, and save the Moreland match factory in Gloucester and its 280 workers from threatened closure.

Moreland, which made England's Glory matches over a century ago, is owned by Bryant & May, owned by Wilkinson Match, one-third owned in turn by Swedish Match, the giant of the business.

Brymay is Britain's only match producer [not quite true – Octavius Hunt of Bristol is still producing today in small quantities]. *Its sales have remained static at around 7.6 million short standards (a short standard is equivalent to 7,200 matches) a year. It produces matches from twenty-one machines, eight of them in Gloucester. Thanks to improvements in machinery and productivity, Brymay could now supply all it sells from the thirteen machines in Liverpool and Glasgow.*

The workers and independents ask why imports, running at about 5.6 million short standards a year, just over 40 per cent of the total demand, cannot be replaced in part by home production. (The cost of imports last year was £4.6m). The independents are further worried because they feel they can buy from only two international giants. Bouldens Match, for instance, developed its business by buying from the Austrian firm Solo – now swallowed up by Swedish match. Last year 3.9 million standards of imports came from Swedish sources, and most of the rest from Russia or Czechoslovakia, whose imports to Britain are all to be handled next year by one concern, the Czech trading agency, Somanco.

It sounds a classic autarchic case for protecting workers and small businessmen against the international monopolists. There are snags. Match production is expensive in Britain, and the wood has to be imported.

A demonstration outside the factory before closure.

Brymay sells as successfully as it does by stressing quality and service. The independents have built their business on price competition, and the promotion of own-label business. So Gloucester could be another potential drain for public funds.

Making sure the press had a good picture.

Even dancing in the street could not save their jobs.

Robert Moreland outside the doomed match factory.

A newspaper cutting in *The Western Daily Press* on
29 January 1976 with headlines: 'The day the lights
go out at a glorious match works.'

The factory, taken from the Bristol Road.

Campaigns were drawn up by the workers and the TUC in an endeavour to keep the factory open, and some demonstrations were held outside the factory. The Co-operative Wholesale Society gave their support, as customers, in favour of Moreland's remaining open. It was suggested, in some quarters, that Bryant & May were illegally importing matches from Sweden through J.J. Masters and then trying to close a UK factory because of over home production for the UK market, and blaming it on foreign imports.

The inevitable happened and after a run of 109 years the factory closed in 1976 with the loss of 280 jobs.

The factory premises reopened as The Moreland Trading Estate in 1978. The one redeeming feature is that the sign outside, which was erected in 1954 at a cost of £500, has been retained.

The company structure in brief form.

1850	Timber importers and joiners	S.J. Moreland & Sons
1890	Sons taken into partnership	S.J. Moreland & Sons
1913 – April	Company registered	S.J. Moreland & Sons Ltd
1913 – September	H. Grimes replaced Philip as director	
1920 – May	G. Moffat as director on death of Grimes	
1920 – November	Henry as director	
1924 – May	Capital share increased to £500,000	

Shareholders were: Harry Moreland with 15,000 existing/7,500 to be allotted
Mabel Grace Grimes with 500/250
Thomas Silvey with 4,848/2,424
Richard Coltman Martin with 3,000/1,500
George Moffat with 25/13
George Leslie Potter and Ernest Arthur Raybould with 248,102/124,051
Frederick William Duart-Smith with 2,000/1,000
John Howe Bourne with 500/250
Emily Moreland with 1,000/500
Henry Moreland with 25/12

This meant that 275,000 of the original shares were taken up and 137,500 of the new shares were being allotted.

1940 – January	George Moffat died. Harry and Henry remained as directors
1956	Henry – chairman, Samuel and Robert as directors
1959 – January	Big financial reshuffle and increase in capital
1966 – April	Change of name to S.J. Moreland & Sons (Holdings) Ltd
1972 – June	Directors were R. Stuart, Samuel and Robert Moreland, and D. Lant
1972 – 21 June	Directors resigned. New directors: G. Kipling, A. Docherty, G. Macfarlane.
1972 – July	Company moved Registered Office to Fairfield Road, Bow, London. (This was when Moreland became a branch of Bryant & May)
1978 – 19 October	Name changed to Wilkinson Match (UK) Ltd. Changes were also made to Memorandum of Association no longer restricting the company to match making but allowing investment in other companies and property.
1978 – December	Office registered at Sword House, Totteridge Road, High Wycombe
1979 – December	Notified registrar that company was a subsidiary of Wilkinson Match Ltd
1980 – 3 October	Allegheny Ludlum Industries Inc. became the ultimate holding company
1981 – May	Name changed to Wilkinson Sword Group (UK) Ltd
1982 – January	By this date Wilkinson Sword Group Ltd was the immediate owner
1982 – September	Registered as a subsidiary of Wilkinson Sword Group Ltd
1985 – November	Ultimate holding company was now Allegheny International Holdings Inc.
1986 – June	Registered office moved to Langley Hall, Station Road, Slough
1987 – February	Registered office moved back to Sword House, High Wycombe
1989 – May	AGM agreed as the company was dormant no auditors would be appointed
1989 – December	Agreed to wind up company and appointed a liquidator. Assets to the value of £1.5m were paid to Wilkinson Sword Ltd

ten

Transport

Transport plays a large part in the success of any industry or commercial enterprise and Gloucester was ideal in many ways.

Although a charter was granted by Queen Elizabeth I giving the city the formal status of a port, few large sea-going ships entered Gloucester because of the tidal and treacherous River Severn. Avonmouth at Bristol continued to be the main port of the estuary.

The idea of a canal was conceived in the 1780s, to develop Gloucester as a port. Eventually all the financial and practical difficulties were overcome and the Gloucester & Berkeley Ship Canal opened in 1827. Boats of over 600 tons that were too large for the canal went to Sharpness docks where the canal started. There they unloaded into lighters for the journey to Gloucester. In the 1880s a new dock was built at Sharpness allowing vessels of 3,000 tons to unload but the larger vessels arriving with timber from the early part of the twentieth century could get only as far as Avonmouth for unloading.

Principal imports over the years were timber, mainly from the Baltic States and Canada, as well as grain. Mills were erected in the dock areas to produce flour and animal feeds. From the 1880s petroleum products, such as benzoline and naphtha, began to arrive, much needed in the area for domestic lighting. Other imports ranged from oranges and lemons, wines and spirits, and bones and guano for fertilisers. Later, imported marble from Italy was worked locally and is often described as enamelled marble.

Return cargoes were not always readily available at Gloucester, except for salt from Worcestershire, so vessels sometimes had to go elsewhere for a return load.

The First World War had a serious effect on trade in Gloucester, with corn imports halved and no timber coming from the Baltic. Trade was still badly depressed into the start of the 1920s and any new industry was well received.

Gloucester Docks, probably just before 1900.

In 1915 Moreland's had worries about the supply of timber and there was an agreement to buy 25,000 cu. ft of southern aspen from the USA the next spring. However, difficulties arose over the chartering of a ship for conveyance and 2,000 cases of more expensive splints were purchased as a short-term measure to last a couple of months. In 1917 poplar from the USA and Scots pine were tried as substitutes. That July, Harry, the chairman's son, was discharged from the army and appointed as buyer of English timber.

For Moreland's, situated adjacent to the canal, the arrival of timber was no problem. Coal came by rail from the nearby Forest of Dean. The river, railways and canals enabled easy distribution of matches to the Midlands and South West.

In September 1873 SJM asked for increased wharf and dock accommodation below Hempstead Bridge. The Dock Company agreed to make a lie-by, large enough to accommodate two large vessels, providing Mr Moreland paid interest on the cost as well as rent for the land. There is no indication as to whether this was actually done.

A year later, during the week ending 14 May, the steamer *Edwards*, having loaded at Kalmar, SE Sweden and skippered by Captain Johansson, docked at Sharpness with a mixed cargo of lathwood and imported Swedish matches for S.J. Moreland. (Presumably Moreland's could not meet demand at this time and imported – as did Bryant & May.)

Sharpness is about half way between Avonmouth and Gloucester at the start of the canal. Timber consignments from Canada in large vessels would unload there while smaller vessels came to Sharpness where they would unload into lighters or dumb barges for the journey to Gloucester.

Moreland's had a motor vessel named *England's Glory*, which was used on the canal and would also tow a dumb barge called *John Bull*, collecting the Canadian poplar unloaded at Sharpness, and taking it to Moreland's Riga Wharf at Hempstead.

The England's Glory barge unloading at the canal side near Moreland's around 1930 when Bill Langford was the engineer on board.

According to Jack Evans, who worked for a company that ran fifty-four barges on the canal, the last cargo of timber came from Canada in 1964, probably from Montreal to Liverpool. This parcel was then loaded into the motor vessel *Sherbourne*, which arrived at Sharpness on 8 April 1964 for unloading into a lighter or barge for delivery up the canal to Moreland's.

During 1898 gold medals were won at Liverpool and Birmingham and a silver at Manchester. England's Glory was now a well-established brand whilst John Bull and Leek (for Wales) were just about to make themselves known. Deliveries were made into Birmingham and the Black Country areas by horse-drawn delivery carts. Although the tilts bore an advertisement on both sides for England's Glory the carts were on a contracted long-term hire.

Mr Cole was born in Gloucester in 1903 and joined the Fire Service in 1918. He remembers, as a child living in Southgate Street, hearing the girls (known as Sammy's Angels after Sam Moreland) clattering down the street at 6 a.m., on their way to work, wearing clogs and shawls.

He used to spend a couple of days a week with the Fire Service, maintaining and cleaning the brasses of the fire ship, *Salamander*, stationed at the docks.

On the other side of the canal from where the fire boat was moored, a large lorry would arrive from Moreland's and unload big cases of matches about the size of a 4ft cube. These were then loaded into narrow boats, which bore the name of Moreland on the aft end. The boats

Horse-drawn delivery carts in the late nineteenth century for deliveries in and around Birmingham and the Black Country.

would travel up the Severn and then the Worcester & Birmingham Canal to a warehouse at 15 Commercial Street, Birmingham, for further distribution to the Midlands. This practice was abandoned in 1954 as the extra loading, unloading and van journeys before and after shipping proved uneconomic.

Crates had been made at the works for some years. They were stencilled with the England's Glory trademark and packed with gross cartons of matches.

Octavius Hunt, a very small manufacturer in Bristol who started about the same time as SJM, used to complain about the quality of the packing cases in which the matches that he purchased from Moreland's were delivered (see below).

In 1942 Moreland's had a log pond on the left of the canal near Two-mile Bend at Hempstead Bridge. John Thornhill recalled that in their younger days it was an ambition of himself and friends to push a log into the canal and 'ride it'. He said they were never able to do so and with hindsight it was probably just as well since it was no doubt a very dangerous thing to try.

In 1919 the first lorry was purchased to start replacing the horse-drawn carts.

In 1931 William Morris sold his first Morris Dictator 5-ton lorry to Moreland's. Its running costs then were 8½d per mile.

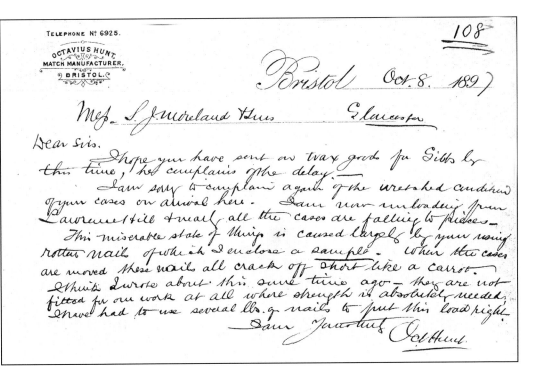

On 8 October 1897 Octavius Hunt of Bristol wrote to Moreland's complaining about the packing cases. 'I am sorry to complain again of the wretched condition of your cases on arrival here. I am now unloading your Lawrence Hill and nearly all the cases are falling to pieces. This miserable state of things is caused largely by your using rotten nails of which I enclose a sample. When the cases are moved these nails all crack off short like carrots. I think I wrote about this some time ago – they are not fitted for our work at all where strength is absolutely needed. I have had to use several lbs of nails to put this load right.'

The Comley family were well represented at Moreland's. All three brothers were drivers whilst Lionel was the family chauffeur, working for fifty-two years. He was the first person outside London to receive an award for forty-five years of safe driving by the Royal Society for Prevention of Accidents. He was fanatical about keeping records of the cars. He was the only person allowed to 'run in' a new car and had a special garage at the works to keep the vehicles in top trim. When short of time he would sometimes only wash the side of the car visible to Mr Harry.

One of Mr Harry's cars in 1924 was a Morris Oxford FH 3386. He was interested in cars and would at times own up to five or six. One of his purchases in 1926 was an American car called a Willys Knight. When the family went away, to Bournemouth, for instance, two cars and two chauffeurs were taken, one for the passengers and one for the luggage. Picnic lunch was always at the same stop and would be laid out from the second car.

Off for their annual outing are the lady employees, or Moreland's Angels, with one man in the charabanc amongst them! The wheels were solid tyres, which would not have been the smoothest of rides as most of the roads were probably gravel. A hood can be just seen on the right, which could be drawn up in the event of rain.

Safe driving awards that were presented to Lionel Comley. The salver was for forty-five years of safe driving from 1927–1971.

During the Second World War one of the cars had a sawdust burning unit attached to the back of the car which Lionel hated. He quite often used to make Mr Harry walk up hills, saying that the car would not get both of them up. Perhaps this was not always strictly true!

Mr Harry must have been fairly fit as he rode a penny-farthing cycle on several occasions to Bournemouth.

He also had a saying: 'When everyone had a Morris I had a Rolls and when most had a Rolls I had a Ford.'

Later in life he also used to say: 'When I was a young man and longed for a whisky I could only afford beer, now I can afford anything and would like a beer I am only able to drink whisky.'

Lionel's other duties during the Second World War involved travelling the country looking for sources of poplar trees for the factory.

Above: The 1926 Willys-Knight imported from the USA.

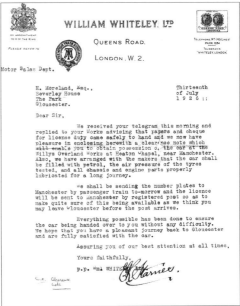

Right: A letter from the agents with details of collecting the new Willys-Knight car.

I understand from his daughter that Lionel and his boss had a lot of time for each other, even though Lionel was not as good a timekeeper as he could have been. At the appointed time Mr Harry would sometimes wait at the roadside for Lionel to arrive and tap his watch while the car was approaching to indicate that Lionel was late. Apparently this had little effect! Mr Harry would send him notes or instructions to 'Mr L.H. Comley', 'Dear Sir', and signed 'Yours faithfully, H. Moreland'.

Tom Davis was the chauffeur for the Moreland family from 1922–1939 and then worked as a driver at the factory from 1946 until retirement in 1975. He used to drive Mr Harry everywhere. Well, nearly everywhere. Sometimes, when leaving Gloucester, whilst driving his boss home to nearby Ross on Wye, Mr Harry would say at Over Bridge, 'Ok Tom, I'll drive now.' So Tom had to get out and walk back to Gloucester. Next morning he had to cadge a lift somehow to Ross on Wye to collect the car and his boss.

(Some of the information given to me regarding the two chauffeurs is slightly conflicting but I have recorded the gist of conversations that seemed reliable at the time.)

Tom Hewlett was a Moreland traveller for South Wales. His widow recounted to me that all the travellers before the war were driven by a chauffeur in a Daimler car carrying a few gross boxes of matches in the back. This practice was set to change, dropping the chauffeurs with the travellers driving themselves, but came to a halt naturally with the onset of war.

Above left: An amusing letter showing the way Harry Moreland wrote to his chauffeur, Lionel.

Above right: Lionel Comley presented with a safe driving award by the Mayor of Gloucester, A.G. Neal.

Opposite below: This picture shows the Moreland fleet in the late 1930s; all Gloucester registered and beautifully turned out. Centre: the big 1931 Morris Commercial K-type eight tonner is a rarity. Based on a bus chassis, the engine and gearbox could be wheeled out on the front axle for maintenance. It was the first real heavyweight from the Morris factory. On the left, the smaller closed lorry is another Morris Commercial; this time the popular 1935 C-type. To the right the glossy flat-bed truck is a 1934 Ford Model BB, usually fitted with a four-cylinder engine but also available with a 30hp V8, which gave enough performance to see off most cars of the time. All three have petrol engines. The diesel was a rarity in the 1930s and diesel pumps were few and far between. The drivers on the left and right are probably brothers, Alec and Ernie Comley, while the centre driver is almost certainly Tom Davis.

It must have been very impressive when a sleek chauffeur-driven Daimler drew up at a post office in a sleepy village and disgorged a smartly dressed man – presumably wearing a dark suit – who then proceeded to try and sell the surprised shopkeeper some cartons of matches.

Mr Harry bought a new Vauxhall car during the war, which was kept at the works, up on blocks, unused for two years, in order to provide extra coupons for petrol that was strictly rationed. No doubt many tricks like this were done all over the country to obtain extra fuel.

David, whose first job from school in 1954 was as a mechanic, later graduated to driver and delivered England's Glory and Safety Matches with pencils to customers. There were also pickups from Bryant & May at Speke, Liverpool, which were mainly matchsticks. Deliveries were made to depots at Pinnal Trading Estate near Exeter, West Wharf at Cardiff and Commercial Street, Birmingham, and he also picked up logs from the Two-mile Bend.

The transport section had about ten or twelve lorries at the time, mostly Commers.

David left Moreland's for another job but did not like it and successfully asked for his job back a week later. He enjoyed it there.

Clary Tranter used to drive a lorry making deliveries of cartons of matches to Moreland's depots at Birmingham, Cardiff and Exeter. The 1950s Sentinel lorry would carry 500 cartons each containing eight gross of matchboxes. He remembers collecting wax, potash and cesquin (probably sesquisulphide of phosphorus), which were stored at the old Standard Match Works.

Left: Tom Davis, driver with Lord Portal. The lorry was first registered in 1956 and was probably a Commer.

Cesquin was an explosive white powder that was mixed in with the match head compo. One employee carried out an unofficial experiment by placing a small amount of cesquin on the ground and hitting it with a spade. The resulting explosion blew a hole in the spade!

After the closure of the match factory, Clary worked over the road in the distribution warehouse for a further eight years. From here items were distributed by Wilkinson Sword such as barbeques, tools, razors and blades, etc. and included matches from the Liverpool factory.

Left: The lorry is thought to be an E.R.F. The drivers are Tom Davis, left, and Clary Tranter.

Left: Lionel Comley sitting on a works van.

Below: Employed from 1937, Mr Ian Oliver must have been one of the smallest commercial van drivers at 3ft 10in tall and drove this 4ft Austin van with a speed limit of 15 mph. It was quite often used for publicity purposes. The miniature van was probably electrically powered and the large van was probably a Morris Commercial.

eleven

Pictorial

In the life of Moreland's match making there must have been hundreds of photographs taken of the works, employees, managers and owners, etc. This chapter will show some of the pictures that I have been able to trace, tending towards what happened at the factory rather than the Moreland family. I have purposely kept to the factory and manufacturing side as this book is not intended to be a family history. Some of the pictures have been reproduced from newspapers or pamphlets and so are not of the best quality.

The first few pictures show some of the factory from about 1900 and then they progress to more modern times.

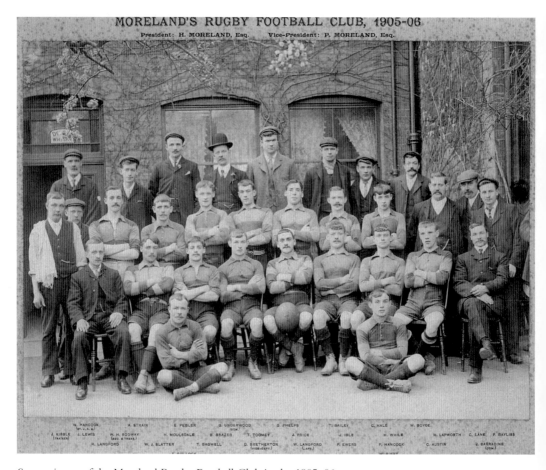

Super picture of the Moreland Rugby Football Club in the 1905–06 season.

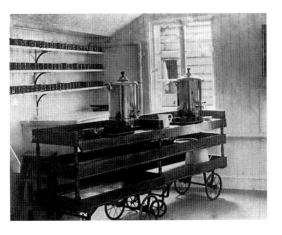

Above left: The 1927 trolley in a corner of the tearoom. Employees were provided each morning (free of charge) with tea and cake.

Above right: Used in the 1930s and '40s on correspondence as a patriotic gesture.

A corner of the label printing department in 1927.

This picture shows one of the factory yards with an interesting vehicle in the background.

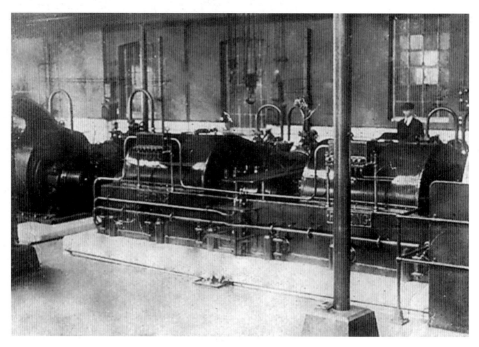

The 400hp engine installed in 1927 – a tribute to the engineering skill of Gloucester engineers, Messrs Fielding & Platt – making England's Glory wheels go round.

Off to their firm's annual staff dinner

The annual staff dinner of Messrs. S. J. Moreland and Sons Ltd. on March 17, 1928, was held in Birmingham. The party was photographed on the LMS station before leaving. From the left, J. Davis, I. C. Pritchard (whose widow loaned the picture), Warmington, J. Ireland, Robinson, J. Barradine, G. E. Evance, G. P. Bunting, F. Davies, R. Berry, W. J. Lewis, L. Smith, T. Moore, T. Hewlett, R. Richardson, F. Smith, R. Hewlett, H. Clarke, W. H. Rodway, R. A. Curtis, L. C. Davis, W. Fisher, F. Hogg, W. J. Courtice, S. Roberts, H. Moss, S. David.

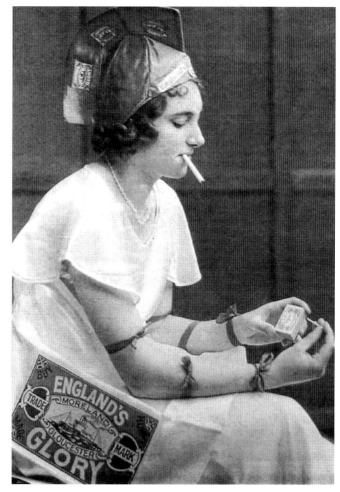

Above: This photograph was taken on the LMS station before leaving for the annual staff dinner held at Birmingham on 17 March 1928. Form the left are: J. Davis, I.C. Pritchard, Warmington, J. Ireland, Robinson, J. Barradine, G.E. Evance, G.P. Bunting, F. Davies, R. Berry, W.J. Lewis, L. Smith, T. Moore, T. Hewlett, R. Richardson, F. Smith, R. Hewlett, H. Clarke, W.H. Rodway, R.A. Curtis, L.C. Davis, W. Fisher, F. Hogg, W.J. Courtice, S. Roberts, H. Moss and S. David.

Right: Miss Molly Smart aged seventeen (later Mrs Davis of Stanley Road, Gloucester), one of the four girls on the match factory float in the Gloucester Carnival procession around 1930. Her colleagues represented John Bull, Jack Tar and Safety Matches – all Moreland brand names. For those worried about such matters, Molly – a non-smoker – was only pretending to light up, a promotional caper for the camera. 'There's no smoke without fire', but in Molly's case there was no smoke at all.

Making the outer section of matchboxes in 1927.

A section of one of the match-making rooms, showing a portion of one of the machines used for making England's Glory matches in 1927.

Machines for cutting match stalks – 70,000 a minute on each machine, photographed here in 1927.

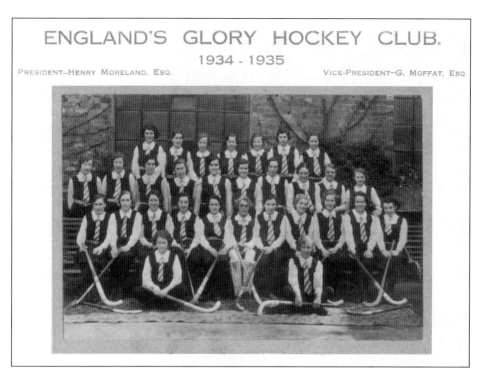

ENGLAND'S GLORY HOCKEY CLUB.
1934 - 1935
PRESIDENT—HENRY MORELAND, ESQ.   VICE-PRESIDENT—G. MOFFAT, ESQ.

Moreland's Hockey Club 1934–35. Centre of the top row is Lillian Cocks, *née* Andrews.

Bristol Exhibition, *c*.1934. The items on the floor were given away for wrappers, etc.

Automatically wrapped gross packets being filled into eight-gross cartons prior to despatch to the warehouse.

Below: The composition from which the match heads were made being mixed in the chemical department.

All dressed up in their furs for an outing in the late 1920s. Vi Neale is on the extreme left. The man in the centre on the right is Mr Berry while the lady between is Elsie Carter (*née* Hawkins). The second lady back from Mr Berry's left shoulder is Lena Turk, with Mr Comley, the chauffeur, on the right.

Thirteen Moreland employees, with over 550 years' service between them, examine the 1867 indenture establishing the match-making concern. Standing, left to right: Mr L.A. Comley, Mr L.H. Comley, Mr E.F. Comley (brothers), Mr S.J. Moreland (managing director), Mr R.K. Marsh, Mr W. Moulsdale, Mr A.E. Woodward, Mr W.E.L. Martin, Mr R. Moreland (works director). Sitting, left to right: Mr J. Price, Mr W.S. Stroud, Mr W.A. Matthews, Mr T. Woodward (whose brother is also in the group).

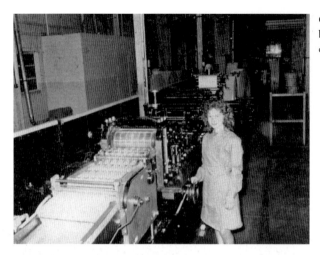

Over a million 'England's Glory' box skillets a day were printed on this Chambon machine.

Left: The delivery point of a high-speed match-making machine where finished matches were automatically punched into the boxes. Each match machine produced approximately 13 million matches a day.

Below: Tests being carried out to comply with the British Standards Institution procedure.

A battery of high-speed machines making inner boxes from reels of cardboard for skillets, which were then conveyed to storage hoppers for delivery to the match-making machines.

Millions of boxes were made and stored in these large bins, ready for use in the match machines.

VISIT OF QUEEN MARY
TO S.J. MORELAND & SONS MATCH FACTORY GLOUCESTER ON 14th OCTOBER 1941

1. 2. 3. 4. 5. 6. 7. H.M. QUEEN 8. 9. 10. 11. 12. 13. 14. 15. 16.
MARY

1. H. HOLMES   4. A.H. BREWER   7. G.A. COLLINS   10. R. WINTLE   13. J.C. PRITCHARD   16. MISS M. PROSSER
2. R. GIFFORD   5. MISS B. HILDICK   8. MISS K. AMPHLETT.   11. MISS V. RASTALL   14. L.C. DAVIS.
3. MISS K. PHILLIPS   6. MISS G. FRANKLIN   9. MISS JONES   12. MISS RUSTELL   15. E.H. SMITH

Harry. Moreland.

Above: The Moreland's staff in this photograph of Queen Mary's visit were identified below in Harry Moreland's handwriting. From left to right: H. Holmes, R. Gifford, Miss K. Phillips, A.H. Brewer, Miss B. Hildick, Miss G. Franklin, G.A. Collins, Miss K. Amphlett, Miss Jones, J.C. Pritchard, Miss V. Rastall, Miss Rustell, L.C. Davis, E.H. Smith, Miss M. Prosser.

Left: Visit of the Duke and Duchess of Beaufort. From right to left: Sam Moreland, Duke of Beaufort, Roy Wood (department foreman), Mrs Moreland, Duchess

Left: Carol Fowke in the printing department in 1973. Also working there at the time were supervisor Ted Goodman from Bryant & May at Bow, Rose Griffiths, Violet Barnes, Geraldine Stock and Tony King.

Below: One of the latest machines for making outer boxes – known as a bar machine – which produced nearly 1,000 outer boxes a minute from printed blanks (skillets). This machine also applied the striking surface.

Above: Late 1930s Moreland's Dance at the Guildhall.

Left: Moreland Cricket Club Dinner and Dance 1963. From left to right: Mrs R. Moreland, ?, Mrs S.J. Moreland, Mr E.E. Brinkworth, Miss E.A. Brinkworth, Mr S.J. Moreland, ?.

Left: Centenary guides at the Moreland's factory in 1967, happily unaware that the factory would close less than a decade later. From left to right: Mr R.T. Baylis (production manager), Mrs P. Powell, Mr R. Wood, Mrs N. Turk, Mrs N. Harvey (welfare officer), Miss R. Barnes, Mrs Beryl Poulton, Mr R. Williams, Mrs P. Williams, Miss S. Turk, Mrs E. Hatherall, Miss S. Smith, Mr W. Martin (vice-chairman of the Works Committee) and Mr T. Woodward.

Above: This picture was taken in the packing department. I remember a lady telling me that she was the girl, aged about fifteen, looking at the camera but I am sorry to say that the name became separated from the picture.

Above right: Albert Galling's retirement. Back row, left to right: Claud Gerrish (wages department), Bob Moreland (works director), Ernest Brinkworth (works manager), Ivan Pritchard (office manager), Sam Moreland (director). Front row, left to right: Roy Galling (son), Albert Galling, Lillian (daughter), Henry Moreland (chairman and managing director), Joan Page (daughter), Royston (grandson), Andrew Page (son-in-law).

Right: Mr E.E. Brinkworth (on the left) congratulates his successor as production manager of the 'England's Glory' match works, Mr R.T. Baylis. In the centre is Mr R. Moreland, a director of the company.

Left: Mrs Gladys Cromwell celebrates her 101st birthday with relatives. Left to right: daughter Doreen Head, daughter-in-law Jean Cromwell, son Anthony Cromwell, daughter-in-law Irene Cromwell and son Richard Cromwell. Mrs Cromwell left school at thirteen to work in the Moreland's factory in Gloucester. During the First World War she worked at an armaments factory in Hempsted before returning to Moreland's, where she worked throughout her marriage to John Cromwell. After she retired she returned briefly to Moreland's in 1974 to make special edition Harlequin matches.

Below: Bliss Museum railway wagon, photographed at the Bliss Museum, Salop, by Jim Stevenson.

Matches

AND....

Match-making.

How an Important
British Industry
was Evolved

"ENGLAND'S GLORY"
A VISIT TO THE
WORKS.

By " Lucifer."

Much of the success of Moreland's as match makers must be attributed to its advertising in the form of hardware and paper ephemera.

This chapter attempts to list and show some of these items. As I am still finding new treasures after many years of collecting Moreland, I am sure that there will be much I have yet to come across and which as a result can not be listed.

–Various fliers from the late 1890s advertising competitions and prizes. (Some examples are shown in Chapter 2.)

–'Matches & Match-making' by Lucifer, published about 1913. (The cover is reproduced opposite.)

–England's Glory Matches c.1929 – an updated version of the above.

–'The Spirit of Whitleyism in Gloucester' – reprinted from *The Citizen* 1923.

–'More Light on a Striking Industry'. (The cover is reproduced opposite.)

–'More Light on a Striking Industry' – another version dated 1930s.

–'The Captains Adventure'.

–'The Revolt of Mr Bleet'.

–Various fliers for distribution to specific towns to encourage the buying of British matches – early 1930s. (Various examples are reproduced towards the end of this chapter.)

–'The Story behind a box of England's Glory' *c.*1958. (The cover is reproduced on page 104.)

–'Merchant Venturers of the Sixties' 1965, printed originally by *Western Daily Press*.

–'Strikes are their Business' – from *600* Magazine 1965–67.

–'The Moreland Story 1867–1967'.

–'Match Making by Moreland's' 1967 – both of these booklets were researched by Brian Frith of Gloucester and printed by Moreland's for their centenary.

Any publicity opportunity that presented itself, or any event that could be used to good advantage, would naturally have had the most made of it. One example of many is the visit of the Bishop of Yukon and his Chaplain to the factory in 1934. (Regrettably the quality of the newspaper picture was not good enough to reproduce here.)

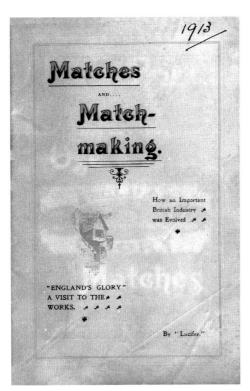

‘Matches & Match-making’ by Lucifer, published 1913. An interesting booklet describing a visit to the England’s Glory works, and with sections on bee keeping, weather, the nursery, health and claiming state pension (as long as your annual income was less than £31.10.0d).

‘More Light on a Striking Industry’, published in 1938, describes a visit to Moreland’s match factory.

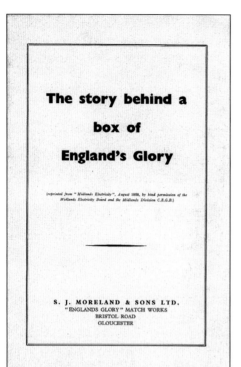

The story behind a

box of

England's Glory

(reprinted from "Midlands Electricity", August 1958, by kind permission of the Midlands Electricity Board and the Midlands Division C.E.G.B.)

S. J. MORELAND & SONS LTD.
"ENGLANDS GLORY" MATCH WORKS
BRISTOL ROAD
GLOUCESTER

Left: The story behind a box of England's Glory', originally printed in 'Midlands Electricity' in 1958, describes the process of producing a box of matches.

Below: Card for constructing a crossword.

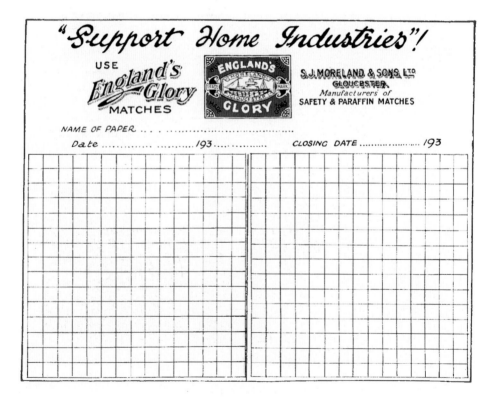

"Support Home Industries"!

USE *England's Glory* MATCHES

ENGLAND'S GLORY

S.J. MORELAND & SONS LTD
GLOUCESTER.
Manufacturers of
SAFETY & PARAFFIN MATCHES

NAME OF PAPER ....
Date .... 193...................   CLOSING DATE 193

Over the years a very varied and huge amount of stationery, envelopes, paper bags and labels, etc. was in everyday use. These can make a most interesting collection on their own.

At least four different whist scorecards were produced as well as a crossword card and a darts scorecard.

Many advertising posters for matches were printed and distributed, made from paper, card, etc. – mostly for use in shops. (Some of these are illustrated in the colour section).

A selection of different whist scoring cards and a celluloid scorer for whist.

Early 1930s trips to Brighton. I wonder if anyone was ever left behind?

Left: Fishing permit on the Wye issued to Jas Boodle in 1939.

Below left: These are images of three pin boxes that are shown flattened to view all surfaces. They contained two boxes of matches and when empty could be used to store odd items such as pins etc.

Below right: A selection of beer mats to advertise Moreland matches.

106

When the factory was cleared out, prior to the site becoming a trading estate, skips of 'stuff', according to local stories, were dumped.

I remember the exhibition put on at the Folk Museum, Gloucester in 1983 when Terry Buss and Derek Saunders had some interesting items displayed. There was also, amongst other things, a large mechanical figure of John Bull exhibited by someone in Gloucestershire. We understood at the time that this person had rescued many items from the factory after closure. No one really seemed to know exactly who he was or where he lived – unfortunately!

Because Moreland's treated its employees just like a large family and organised outings, the works trips must have been very exciting and made a dramatic change. What a difference from the works a day in Margate or Brighton must have been, when the train disgorged its Gloucester crowd onto the platform ready for a charabanc trip until lunch. Afterwards there was probably a chance to paddle in the sea! Woe betide you if you got lost or did not have your ticket for the return journey!

Above left: In 1930 half the works went to Brighton and the other half to Margate. Could you choose?

Above right: Back of a pack of pre-war John Bull playing cards.

Although I have collected match labels and boxes from the age of eleven and lived within ten miles of Gloucester until National Service, it never occurred to me either to visit the works or send to them for some labels. Other people often made use of this service, however, according to some correspondence I have seen, until the works ceased this practice in the late 1960s.

The company also supplied a free life insurance policy for employees, which provided, in 1926, ten pounds for each year of service to a maximum of two hundred pounds. I was given, after her death, papers belonging to Vera Rastall, connected with her time at Moreland's. Included were wage slips and letters to and from the management in relation to her duties as a trade union representative. Apart from making interesting reading, they give another insight into the management's care for the well-being of its employees, perhaps an attitude that the much of of present-day industry could learn from.

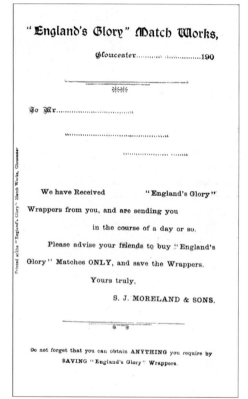

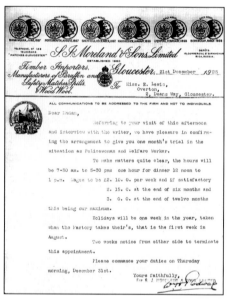

Above right: 1925 letter of engagement to Miss Lewis as policewoman and welfare worker who later left and obtained a position as assistant matron at the Home of Hope in 1935.

Left: Interesting receipt for wrappers.

Every employee had insurance provided.

The patriotic fliers that were distributed around towns and cities, mostly in the Midlands, were quite imaginative. They all endeavoured to promote the purchase of British goods, namely matches. Nowadays we import even more and seem to have lost a sizeable chunk of our manufacturing ability, and so have become, or are fast becoming, a throwaway nation.

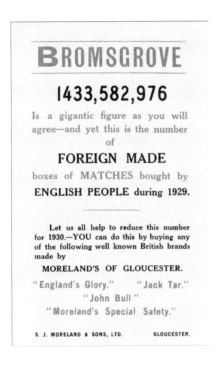

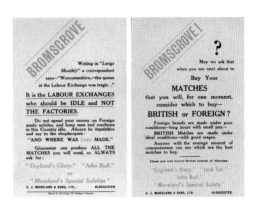

Above: Two flyers for Bromsgrove.

Left: One of a series of flyers in the late 1920s and early '30s, mostly distributed in the Midlands. British firms did their best to curb the ever-increasing imports of foreign matches by local advertising.

Four flyers for the Midlands.

Above left: Four flyers for the South Midlands.

Above right: Four flyers of the late 1920s to early 1930s.

Left: 1967 Centenary Celebrations invitation.

Below: Menu for the Seventh Annual Pensioner's Reunion in 1975.

thirteen

Miscellaneous

No doubt industrial espionage, or exchange of information to put it more mildly, always has and still does take place in industry. I have two lots of correspondence on these lines, which I find fascinating.

In the first batch of letters the correspondence is difficult to understand fully because it is a copy of letters from one party to another, without the replies being available.

In 1930 letters were flying between J. John Masters, Bryant & May and Moreland concerning a firm called Ouse Traders Ltd, which imported safety and paraffin matches from Belgium. The firm was also reported to have purchased a parcel of land near Kings Lynn in order to build a match factory. This later proved to be untrue, as it was only an enquiry to the local council and the piece of land concerned turned out to be partly a playing field and allotments. At the same time a certain Mr Merckx had expressed an interest to the Belgian Chamber of Commerce in London for a match factory at Kings Lynn.

A quote from one letter a week later said, 'Merckx would be able to supply machinery from Belgium, but we do not think he can find much cash at the present time. If there really are men of means behind the project, the next point is to consider how best to "get at" them to try and persuade them to drop it.'

In another letter it was said that some information had come from 'a certain Mr Freedman, a Polish Jew of a low type who runs a bazaar in one of the poorest parts of London.' He reported that one of the main men to put up the money for this factory was the Mayor. So an agent was engaged to dig out information on the Mayor (of Kings Lynn) who turned out to be a chemist.

A certain amount of confusion reigned at this point but a later letter revealed the truth. It was the Lord Mayor of London who was to be the possible financier for the match factory! Needless to say it was all a storm over nothing as the factory was never built.

(Merckx & Co. were listed as a Belgian match company, which closed in 1974 – taken over by Sweden (sic).

The second batch of letters all came from a William Lee who was obviously in the employ of Harry Moreland to find out what he could about the Anglia Match Co. Ltd at Letchworth.

54 Gernon Road, Letchworth
27 April 1939

Harry Moreland Esq

Sir,
Today I left Gloucester at 8.20am, arrived here at 1pm and so far find that about 100 people (25 men and about 75 girls) are employed at the Anglia match works. The foreman is paid about £5.00 per week, the labourers ⅓d to ⅕d per hour.
The manager is a Mr Girching, an Austrian. I have got in touch with a man who is willing to help me. He is under the impression that it is for a trade union. I will report progress tomorrow, the 28th. I will endeavour to get the girls' wages.
I am Sir, Yours faithfully, William C. Lee

28 April 1939

Sir,
Today I have made further enquiries and find that girls 14 years of age are paid 18/- per week, 17 years £1.7.0d and 18 years £1.12.0d per week less insurance. They work from 8am to 5.45pm each day

except Saturdays when they do not work, except when they are busy. No matter what kind of work they all receive the same pay according to age. Labourers are paid 1s 2d per hour, boys 10½d per hour. There are two mechanics who act as foremen who are paid about £5.0.0 per week.

There are four veneer machines, two boys and two girls act as runners off. On average they make 100 cartons of 16 gross per day.
I am Sir, yours faithfully…

29 April 1939

Sir,
After posting my report yesterday, I called upon Miss Rees, organiser of the National Union of General and Municipal Workers who informed me that the manger of the Anglia Match Co. was strictly carrying out the rates and conditions of the National Joint and Industrial Council, and was paying wages slightly above the local rates. Also that some time ago the manager said that he wishes entirely to comply with all the rates of the match making industry. One of the employees acts as Shop Steward for the Union, and one of the clerks collects the weekly contributions.

The office staff consists of three females, secretary and welfare, wages clerk and despatch clerk.

They have no transport vehicles, all the conveying of goods being done by the railway company, L&NR. They do very little trade in Letchworth and sell their matches at 8½d per dozen wholesale. All around the building is very untidy with waste.

On Saturday 29th inst. I left Letchworth at 2.35pm, arriving Gloucester at 7.10pm.
I am Sir, yours faithfully…

Cornish pilot gigs

Why gigs in a book on matches? Patience – all will be revealed.

Before 1880 pilot gigs were used to meet incoming sailing vessels for orders, piloting and general communications. Records show that they were also used for racing as far back as the 1820s – pre-RNLI lifeboats.

Use of gigs after 1880 declined as sails and oars gave way to engines and many gigs were either left to rot or broken up. Not so at Newquay and the Scilly Isles, where they were kept and raced. Racing was suspended during the First World War after which the gigs were not required for piloting, as cargo ships ceased to visit Newquay Harbour. After a fire at the store in Newquay, the gigs were bought by the town for £5 each and in 1921 a rowing club was formed. In 1953 the trustees of the club were invited to the Isles of Scilly to purchase the remaining gigs there.

The Treffry Company of Newquay ordered a new gig in 1938 with the instruction that she was to be the fastest. She was the longest, at 32ft, that the Peter family ever built but her beam was still only 4ft 10in. Once she struck the South Pier at Newquay at full speed and only suffered slight damage to the bow. She was also filled by a ground sea in 1955 in the harbour where a lesser boat would have been smashed to pieces.

She proved to be a very fast gig and one of the finest in heavy seas.

After the battering in 1955, the club could not stop her leaking and it was decided a new keel was necessary. The search for a good piece of clean timber 32ft long proved a problem. A piece of suitable oak, narrow-leaf elm or American rock elm, of this length, could not be found. Mr Henry Moreland with his knowledge of the timber trade took up the search. After some weeks he found a baulk at the Castletown Sawmills, Stafford. The tree had come from the Clanna Estate in Gloucestershire. Mr Moreland advised them to take enough for all of the keels of the pilot gigs as this length of oak was so unusual. The cut piece of timber weighed 9cwt.

Mr Moreland had only seen one gig race but was very impressed by the stamina of the crews taking part. Writing to the club for final arrangements of delivery he said: 'I shall be very glad if you will accept the baulk and the delivery charge as some little token of esteem and respect for the men who, in these changing days, find interest, sport and pleasure in the pilot gigs, and the welfare of the Newquay Rowing Club.'

In 2004 Robert Moreland attended by invitation and proudly presented the awards to the winning crews at the annual regatta at Newquay.

Newquay harbour in 1895 with four gigs, Dove, Treffry, Teaser (ex Zoe Treffry) and Newquay.

Newquay Harbour 1895 with 4 gigs,
Dove, Treffry, Teaser (ex Zoe Treffry) & Newquay

Below: Newquay harbour, June 1955. Beached left to right: *Treffry, Slippen, Golden Eagle, Shah.* Afloat left to right: *Bonnet, Dove, Newquay.*

Wrappers and packet labels

This book would be very incomplete without a brief mention of wrappers and packet labels.

Should they have been included in the labels or ephemera section? Maybe. They are an important part of many match collections but, like the matchboxes, were made to be thrown away when the packet was ripped open.

I show here only a few examples from the dozens that were printed in the life of the company.

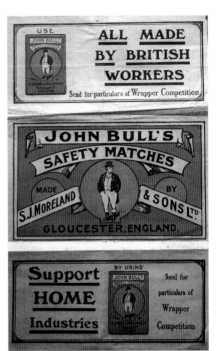

Above: Part of an early wrapper, *c.*1900.

*Above right: c.*1920s John Bull wrapper.

Below right: Used from 1965–71. Although the price of a box of matches remained at this price until decimalisation, the contents dropped from 54 to 41 over this period.

Below: Moreland Safety Match wrapper.

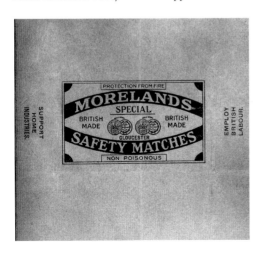

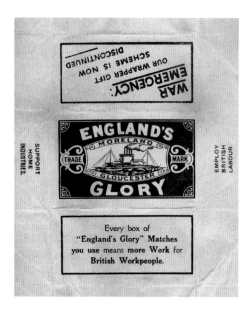

Above: Wartime emergency wrapper.

Right: The age of this newspaper cutting is not known. In the centre of the booklet 'The story behind a box of England's Glory' (published in 1958) Mr Moreland mentions that he would like to know the origin of the ship on the England's Glory boxes. It seems amazing the firm did not know this when the framed poster *c.*1900–10 (see cover of this book) had HMS *Devastation* printed in the picture.

Below: An enamelled metal sign 12 x 6in with dark blue lettering on white.

MATCHED

A. STURGESS, Springfield Road, Gillingham, Kent, writes:

COULD you give me any information about the ship which appears on the boxes of England's Glory matches?

It looks to me as if the name on it is the HMS Devastation.

★ **Devastated to tell you, but there isn't much known.**

The British Matchbox Label Society, experts in the matter, say there is quite a dispute about it.

Some claim it does read "HMS Devastation", others say you can't tell.

Either way, we can find no record of any Royal Navy ship of that name.

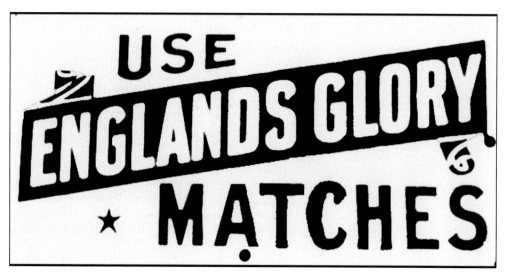

The Gloucester Match Company

William Taylor, a Gloucester man who had learnt the art of match making in Birmingham, was appointed foreman to the new match works of Samuel Moreland in 1867. This was the beginning of an important new industry in Gloucester.

Four years later, slate merchants Henry Belcher and Joseph Gee started matchmaking as a sideline to their business, also with William Taylor, who by this time had left Morelands as their manager. Soon afterwards they had sold the business to Henry Arnold and Thomas Gee (elder brother of Joseph).

A serious fire virtually destroyed the whole works in 1872 and after a short while William Taylor started on his own account, retiring from matchmaking in 1880. Meanwhile Thomas Gee bought out Arnold in April 1873, rebuilt the works and continued the business until 1881, producing thirteen different brands of matches which are now very rare indeed.

Morelands continued expanding on the match front, eventually giving up the timber and joinery side of the business.

Henry Cowles was listed as a matchmaker in 1877. But it is believed that he never made matches and was only listed because he took over Tredwell's Yard when Moreland vacated the premises.

Standard Match Co. started in 1921 and was purchased by Morelands in 1926, continuing to produce until 1938.

The only other name of a match company or business in Gloucester that has surfaced in any public or newspaper records is the little known Gloucester Match Company. Not much is known about the Gloucester Match Company, in spite of many futile hours of research on my part. What is known is that the company registered 'British Made Matches, "As used by Conn"', on 8 March 1911. The address was given as Bristol Road, Gloucester. Since this vague address equals that of Morelands and no other match firm was then operating, Morelands were obviously the Gloucester Match at this time.

The use of the name petered out when Bryant & May took the control of Morelands in 1913. The grey area is the formation of The Gloucester Match Co. When did the company start and who formed it?

On 10 April 1873 Thomas Gee, superintendent of the Hardwicke Reformatory near Gloucester, bought out his partner, Henry Arnold, governor of the Manchester and Salford Reformatory, and took over the lease of the City Match Works. (The Gee family came from the Manchester area and Joseph Smith Gee, younger brother of Thomas, had a wife, Sarah, from Salford, thus providing the link with Henry Arnold.).

The company produced thirteen known brands including England's Glory and Monstre Matches. England's Glory was certainly one of the earlier brands whilst Monstre Matches (Zulu King) was most probably inspired by the hostilities which broke out between Britain and the Zulus in 1879.

On 27 February 1875 Thomas Gee surrendered the City Match Works lease, and on 1 March a new fourteen-year lease was agreed, at £50 per annum, between Thomas Gee, Bernard Edwards and the landlords of the match site. (This rather suggests that Bernard Edwards became a partner?)

Mr Brian Frith, the Gloucester historian who wrote the centenary booklets for Morelands, has said that Morelands took over the business of Thomas Gee & Co. in 1881. This information came from his step-grandmother, who was a daughter of Joseph Smith Gee.

Gloucester Match produced an England's Glory label, at first glance the same as the Gee version, apart from the maker's name. There are, however, small differences in the floral design and the ship's rigging. Also produced was the Monstre Match label which, once again, appears to be the same as the Gee label in all but the maker's name.

Were the Gloucester Match versions produced by Morelands after the acquisition of Gee? Or produced by Gee alongside its own labels after Edwards joined the company? Or were they produced by Morelands either by arrangement with, or were the designs lifted from, Gee?

At this stage I am inclined to think that Gee and Edwards started the Gloucester Match Co. about 1879/80 with the Monstre Match. Unfortunately, in a difficult situation there is always something else to cloud the issue.

The Shaughraun is the name of a theatrical production, a play which opened in London during September 1875, its setting being County Sligo on the west coast of Ireland seven years earlier. Boucicault, the author, played Conn (the title character), the shaughraun or vagabond (in Irish 'seachran' means wandering), who roams with his dog and peaked cap as far afield as Australia in search of his heart-wish. (One of Boucicault's plays was performed in London during 2005.)

Following the great success in 1875 of the Shaughraun in London, Boucicault petitioned Prime Minister Disraeli, in the name of his audience, to release all Irish political prisoners. Predictably, the lack of response was deafening and a current view emerged that the petition was just a publicity stunt.

Apparently almost all of his plays were lavish and epic melodramas which pandered to a then largely illiterate mass audience's appetite for spectacle and sensation. Eventually the fashion passed; Boucicault died in 1890, already half-obscure, but he had created a thing of lasting value in the three comedy dramas with uninhibited Gaelic titles set in Ireland: Colleen Bawn, 1860; Arragh-na-Pogue, 1864; and the Shaughraun,1874.

So the complication is that match labels produced on a topical subject had to be out on sale shortly after the event. This means that the Shaughraun Match must have been on sale in 1875 or early 1876. Likewise, the very similar box produced by Moreland must have been issued at roughly the same time.

Could Moreland, Gee and Edwards have started the Gloucester Match as a joint venture? We will probably never know all the details.

When Moreland bought out Gee in 1881, I am certain he also owned Gloucester Match Co. – and it may have been owned by him even earlier. Gloucester match brands Skipper and John Bull of the 1890s were also Moreland brands at the same time.

The John Bull skillets are identical to the Moreland versions. They were probably all produced before or about the time when Moreland registered the brand on 22 February 1898.

The design of the Gloucester Skipper Match is very similar to the British Skipper, which was also produced in a red on white and a black on yellow version by Moreland. Incidentally, there is a real likeness between the Gloucester Skipper and the Birmingham Congreve Match (which I have just included for interest).

We now come to the British Made Matches. This was a brand produced by Moreland as an ARTB and a skillet some time after 1900. Later the design was used by the Standard Match and the Midland Match Co.'s, once they became part of the Moreland Group. The example shown with the hand-written panel is identical to a Moreland version and the writing is that of Mr Harry Moreland (according to Henry Moreland, says Ivan Pritchard in a letter to Dick Holton in 1948).

Above left: Gee England's Glory. Seemingly first produced in 1872 by Arnold, Gee & Co.; colour: magenta on white.

Above right: G.M England's Glory; colour: magenta on white.

Monstre Matches, probably inspired by
hostilities which broke out between
Britain and the Zulus in 1879. Colour:
black on yellow. An almost identical label
was also produced by the Gloucester
Match Company.

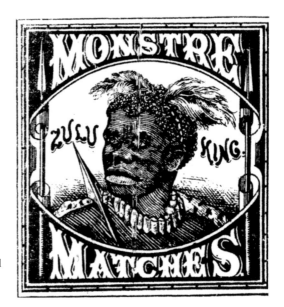

The other example of 'As used by Conn' was registered in 1911 by The Gloucester Match Co., Bristol Road, Gloucester. This must be Morelands, although I still cannot positively link Morelands to the Gloucester Match.

Whether or not Moreland was always the owner of Gloucester Match Company I feel is unclear and it remains a matter for speculation. I leave you to decide this on the circumstantial evidence presented.

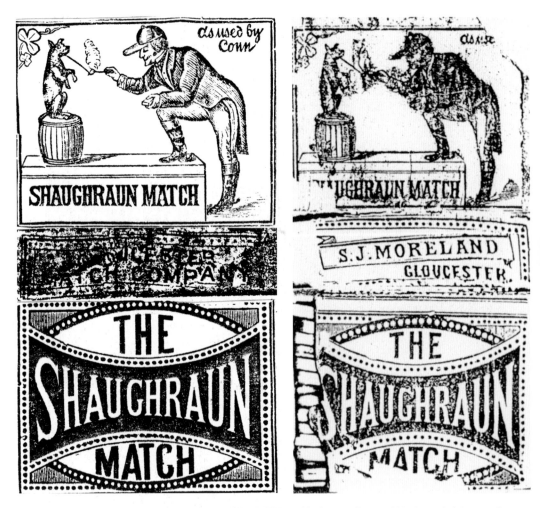

Above left: Shaughraun; issued *c.*1875 as a topical label. Colour: black on yellow and black on dark brownish paper. Two varieties: one with twenty-five spots up the side vertically and thirty-one across and above match – excluding side row. Second version is twenty-nine and forty.

Above right: Moreland Shaughraun; this label has twenty-five vertical spots and probably thirty-one across. The picture is made up from a very scruffy box found in Wigan and its colour is black on yellow; again, it is from around 1875.

Above left: Skipper G. Match; colour: purple/brown on off-white.

Above right: British Skipper; S.J. Moreland & Sons (before 1913). In two colours: crimson on white and black on yellow.

Birmingham Congreve: slate blue on white. I think it has many similarities to the Skipper Match. It was probably from around the 1870s. Manufacturer?

Above left and right: British Made Matches, colour: blue on white. Printed 1908. The words in centre panel are reproduction of the handwriting of Mr Harry Moreland, managing director.

British Made Matches (Conn); colour: blue on off-white. Registered 8 March 1911.

Although the reproduction of these examples is poor I thought their inclusion was justified on account of their extreme rarity. The deterioration of quality is perhaps understandable given that they were printed directly onto cardboard using cheap, unstable and highly evanescent inks designed to last a week or two rather than a century plus.

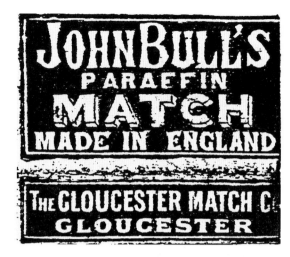

John Bull. 1) colours: blue/green on white, red on white.

John Bull. 2) colour: red on white.

John Bull. 3) colour: brick red on white.

Some new labels, hitherto generally unknown, discovered immediately prior to printing.

A) Black on buff, 1870's. B) Black on yellow, 1870's. C) Magenta on white, c1879.
D) Black, yellow on buff, 1890's

A

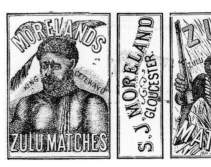

B

C

D

Rosewood Match. In red and green on off-white and red
and black on yellow.

These two labels were recently discovered together with the
old labels on page 126 opposite. They have been included
here although they do not seem to have the same style and
indeed most old Moreland labels usually included the word
Gloucester.

Other titles published by Tempus

Haunted Gloucester
EILEEN FRY AND ROSEMARY HARVEY

Gloucester's historic docks have some strange stories to tell and the city's twelfth-century cathedral also has its secrets. From a ghostly procession at Berkeley Castle to the Grey Lady at the Theatre Royal, this new and fascinating collection of strange sightings and happenings in the city's streets, churches and public houses is sure to appeal to anyone intrigued by Gloucester's haunted heritage.

07524 3312 1

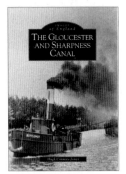

Gloucester and Sharpness Canal, The
HUGH CONWAY-JONES

This collection of 200 photographs graphically illustrates the changing role of the Gloucester & Sharpness Canal and the docks at each end, starting with the era of the sailing ship, continuing with the heyday of the steamer and concluding with the trend from commercial to leisure use.

0 7524 1709 6

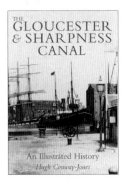

Gloucester & Sharpness Canal: A History
HUGH CONWAY-JONES

When the Gloucester & Sharpness Canal opened in April 1827, it was the widest and deepest canal in England, capable of taking most of the largest seagoing ships of the day. Drawing on contemporary sources, Hugh Conway-Jones sheds new light on the difficulties encountered in its construction, including the junction with the Stroudwater Canal, the only intersection of two independent canals in the country.

0 7524 2789 X

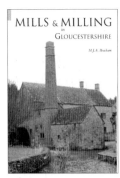

Mills and Milling in Gloucestershire
MICHAEL BEACHAM

Despite their central role in society, we know comparatively little about individual corn mills until the seventeenth century, possibly because water mills and later windmills were such a common sight, so much used by everyone, that details were unnecessary. This book strives to put that to rights, documenting the varied mills of Gloucestershire.

07524 3459 4

If you are interested in purchasing other books published by Tempus, or in case you have difficulty finding any Tempus books in your local bookshop, you can also place orders directly through our website

www.tempus-publishing.com